Robert Nozick

Key Contemporary Thinkers

Robert Nozick

Property, Justice and the Minimal State

JONATHAN WOLFF

Stanford University Press
Stanford, California

Stanford University Press
Stanford, California
© 1991 Jonathan Wolff
Originating publisher: Polity Press, Cambridge
In association with Basil Blackwell, Oxford
First published in the U.S.A. by
    Stanford University Press, 1991

Cloth ISBN 0-8047-1855-5
Paper ISBN 0-8047-1856-3
LC 90-70906
This book is printed on acid-free paper

Contents

Preface

I first read Nozick as an undergraduate in 1980. At that time philosophy students usually reacted to *Anarchy, State, and Utopia* in one of two ways. Either they thought its conclusions so repugnant that it should not be taken seriously as political philosophy at all, or they thought its conclusions so repugnant that it was vital (but not very difficult) to show how it fails. Now, in 1990, as a teacher of philosophy, I still encounter these two reactions, but fairly often I also encounter a third: that, broadly speaking, Nozick is right.

My own initial entanglement with Nozick was slightly more complicated. Feeling a strong attraction to individual liberty, and being prepared to believe that a likely consequence of this might well be some form or other of anarchism, I had attempted some preliminary reading into anarchist theory. But I was both dissatisfied with the uncritical vagueness of anarchy's defenders and annoyed by the crass, one-line dismissals of it by its opponents. So I welcomed the chance to read a book with 'Anarchy' in its title as part of my introduction to political philosophy. However, I had taken it for granted that the anarchy referred to would be socialist, or, at the least, egalitarian, and, as I read Nozick, I became increasingly concerned. What was money doing in the state of nature? And private property rights? And free enterprise? It had not even occurred to me that anarchy could be made to yield rampant capitalism. An initial commitment to liberty seemed to lead, not to equality, as I had assumed, but to inequality. Thus I was forced, for the first time, to face the question of whether I cared more about liberty than equality. I had no firm answer to that question then, and I have no firm answer now. However, as I aim to show here, Nozick, despite his best efforts, does not, in fact, succeed in demonstrating any important inconsistency between liberty and equality. So I can, at least for the time being, put off the question.

I cannot, however, put off the questions of why it is I think Nozick is wrong, and why it is important to show that he is wrong. Fortunately, the second question, at least, has an easy answer. Nozick's views have many affinities with the defence of *laissez-faire* capitalism which has been part of the 'ruling ideology' of the 1980s. It has not escaped my notice that during my entire university career – both as student and teacher – Margaret Thatcher has been Prime Minister of Great Britain, and ideas like those of Nozick have had, to put it mildly, a huge and destructive effect on the lives of a great many people. It is, perhaps, unlikely that showing the difficulties with those ideas will have much practical effect, yet the task is still worthwhile.

My intention has been to present my case by reason, not rhetoric. This accounts for much of the style and tone of this book. One easy way of writing about Nozick would be in the denunciatory mode of a political pamphlet, revealing outrage after outrage. I wanted to avoid that at all costs, for this is intended to be a work of political philosophy, not polemic. I have tried to set out Nozick's views as fairly as possible – adding extra arguments where I can – and then to show, coolly and calmly, where Nozick is mistaken. Finally, this is a book about Nozick, not about me. Although I have grappled with Nozick partly as a means towards learning the truth for myself, the point of this book is not to display my own views, but to examine Nozick's.

The opportunity to do this came when Mike Rosen suggested that I should write this book. The idea that *someone* should write a book on Nozick was John Thompson's. I am very grateful to them both for setting me off on this project, and for their encouragement along the way. Lively discussions with Mike, and his perceptive comments on the penultimate manuscript, have also led to many improvements. Jerry Cohen, who first introduced me to *Anarchy, State, and Utopia*, and convinced me of its importance, also provided immensely helpful comments on the whole manuscript, and of course, his own work on Nozick has been a major influence on mine (as it has been on so many). Others who have read the work in various stages, and from whose suggestions and criticism I have profited, include Jonathan Dick, Chris Hull, Miles Sabin, Nick Zangwill, and, especially, Simon Evnine and Elaine Collins. I would also like to thank two anonymous publisher's readers for their useful suggestions, and Malcolm Budd for his help and encouragement.

My greatest debt in writing this book, however, is to Bill Hart. We have spent innumerable hours talking about the issues discussed here, and at every stage Bill has provided detailed notes on draft after draft. So many of Bill's suggestions have found their way into the final version that there is no doubt that his presence can be found on almost every page of this book. Perhaps the only thing that has resisted his influence is the title. And that came from John Thompson.

Acknowledgements

Excerpts from *Anarchy, State, and Utopia* are reprinted by permission of the publishers, Basic Books, Inc, New York, and Basil Blackwell, Oxford, and are copyright © 1974 by Basic Books, Inc.

Note on References

Numbers in parentheses in text, e.g. (56), refer to page numbers of Robert Nozick's *Anarchy, State, and Utopia* (Blackwell, Oxford, 1974). References in footnotes to John Locke's *Second Treatise* are given by section number, rather than by page numbers of any particular edition.

Introduction

For almost two decades, debate in analytical political philosophy has been dominated by two highly contrasting works: John Rawls's *A Theory of Justice*, and Robert Nozick's *Anarchy, State, and Utopia*. Rawls, in 1971, presented the case for a form of liberal egalitarianism, while Nozick, in 1974, argued for libertarianism – the free market, absolute property rights, and the 'minimal state'. A vast quantity of critical literature has been generated in response to both Rawls and Nozick, but unlike Rawls, Nozick has won few followers among academic political philosophers. Nevertheless, in practical political terms we have, in the last decade or so, seen a move away from the left-wing welfarism defended by Rawls. It is Nozick who seems closer to the political spirit of the present age.

The two works are strikingly different in style, as well as in content. Few would say that Rawls is an easy writer to read, and *A Theory of Justice* is written in a careful, qualified manner which makes it, by Rawls's own admission, 'a long book not only in pages'.[1] *Anarchy, State, and Utopia*, on the other hand, is self-consciously 'flashy' and deliberately provocative. Nozick seems always to find the brilliant example, the memorable turn of phrase. Part of his declared purpose is to unsettle the reader, and depending upon one's mood *Anarchy, State, and Utopia* can often be amusing or annoying to read. But it is always engaging.

Perhaps significantly, Rawls's project in political philosophy is clearly his life's work. Not only did he publish a number of important papers leading up to *A Theory of Justice*, but in the last twenty years he has continued to publish substantial developments and further defences of his views, taking up and answering or acknowledging the most important criticism. For Nozick, however, political philosophy has taken up only a few years of his academic life. Since *Anarchy, State, and Utopia* he has barely returned to the subject, and so his critics remain unanswered. Nozick's attention has, more recently, been given over to many other topics, some of which are represented in his huge and eclectic *Philosophical Explanations*, published in 1981. This work ranges over problems in the philosophy of mind, ethics, epistemology, and metaphysics, and the sections of the book on knowledge and scepticism have in particular received a great deal of critical attention. Subsequently Nozick has worked on topics such as Indian philosophy, spiritual leaders, and the nature of wisdom. Only in his most recent book, *The Examined Life*, published in 1989, has Nozick discussed again some of the themes of *Anarchy, State, and Utopia*. Here Nozick briefly indicates that he has modified his views, and no longer considers himself a libertarian. For now, however, in so far as political philosophy is concerned, the words 'Nozick' and 'libertarianism' remain inextricably linked.

In this work I shall concentrate on an examination of *Anarchy, State, and Utopia*, although Nozick's other writings will be discussed where they are relevant to his political philosophy. Part of my task will be to reconstruct Nozick's arguments and conclusions to make them as coherent as possible. This is not always a simple matter, for Nozick's intellectual enthusiasm shows itself in a tendency to take up at length any interesting side issue, and thus it is not always clear what is the argument and what the digression.[2] Further, vital premises of arguments can be scattered over many pages, or missing entirely, and Nozick makes little attempt to summarize or clarify his arguments, or, often, even to show how the separate parts are related. This is partly a consequence of Nozick's decision to present a 'philosophical exploration of issues' rather than a full-scale philosophical treatise. Thus he offers only an outline of his theory; an outline which, in many respects, still remains to be filled in. Thus I shall try to clarify Nozick's reasoning and make good the gaps where necessary and possible, so that we might appreciate the force of the arguments, and subject them to rigorous examination. One cost of this approach is that, inevitably, many of Nozick's fascinating contributions to moral and political philosophy, such as his case for vegetarianism, and his assault on the deterrence theory of punishment, must remain undiscussed here. However, I hope the benefits of a clear view of the main arguments make this sacrifice worthwhile.

To understand the significance of Nozick's project it is necessary to set it against competing approaches to the problems of political philosophy. One task of the political philosopher is to take values appropriate to the political sphere, such as liberty, equality, happiness, and freedom from need, and to examine their inter-relations. Are these values compatible or do they exclude each other? Does the achievement of one bring with it the achievement of another? What should we do if and when these values conflict? Some political theorists, like the utilitarians, claim that one value is fundamental, and the other values are at best secondary or derivative.[3] Other theorists argue for a plurality of ultimate values, and these plural theories come in two forms. Some allow a hierarchy of values, so that, even where independent values clash, there will be a determinate answer to the question of which one, politically, should be preferred. Rawls, for example, admits the independent value of both civil liberty and economic equality, but he argues that any conflict between them should be dealt with by giving civil liberty priority. On the other hand, some theorists judge that there can be ineliminable conflicts of value.[4] These 'conflict' theorists suggest that sometimes there simply is no determinate answer to the question of what should be done when certain values collide.

In expecting more of political philosophy than the conflict theorists, hierarchical pluralists have the additional task of explaining how there can be more than one fundamental value, without these ever issuing in insoluble conflicts. Single-value theories seem in a way more elegant and more powerful, promising a decision procedure to cover every situation, basing every decision on fundamentally the same grounds. Given these advantages, it is not surprising that the burden of establishing a single-value theory is a heavy one. The selected value has first to be shown to be of overwhelming fundamental importance, and second, must not itself generate insoluble conflicts. So, for example, the utilitarian argues that happiness is the sole good, and that we should be interested only in maximizing quantities of happiness.

Part of the argument of this book is that we should see Nozick as presenting, at root, a single-value political philosophy, based, not on happiness, like the utilitarian, nor on liberty, as one might expect from a libertarian, but on absolute property rights: rights of ownership over oneself and over things in the world. No one has the right to interfere with your person or your possessions unless either you have consented, or you have forfeited your rights by violating the rights of others. Your right to liberty is simply a consequence of this right to self-ownership. This, Nozick seems to suggest, is enough to settle all disputes that properly fall within the political sphere. If Nozick can show that property rights deserve the importance they are given within his theory, and that they do not themselves issue in irresolvable conflicts, then he will have given us everything we could hope for in a political philosophy. He will have established a simple, single decision procedure to cover every political problem.

In order to locate Nozick's views within the broader context of political philosophy we can think of him as following a tradition of political thought, best referred to as the natural-rights individualist tradition. Locke is often taken to be the first major advocate of this type of view, and Locke's influence on Nozick runs deep. It is not absurd to see Nozick's project as an attempt to rehabilitate what he regards as the rational core of Locke's political philosophy. But this is not to say that Nozick takes over Locke entire: there are many important modifications and some major disagreements. At some of these points Nozick finds help from other broadly individualist writers, and so in explaining Nozick's views it will often be illuminating to look at the writings of allies and opponents from both inside and outside the individualist tradition. In so doing we will be able to appreciate Nozick's work as a development of an established, but until very recently, largely neglected, political theory; indeed one so neglected that Richard Tuck has recently written that 'With the exception of Robert Nozick, no major theorist in the Anglo-Saxon world for almost a century has based his work on the concept of a right.'[5] One of the many merits of Nozick's work is that it has put this approach to political philosophy back into the mainstream of philosophical debate.

Nozick's project is to defend the libertarian minimal state – akin to the 'nightwatchman' state of classical liberalism – which exists purely to safeguard the personal and property rights of individuals. The enterprise falls into three stages. First, against the Anarchist, Nozick puts the case that a state at least as extensive as the minimal state is justified. Second, against the defender of the extensive state,

Nozick argues that the minimal state is the most extensive form of legitimate state. From these claims, of course, it follows that the minimal state is the only justified form of state, and the third stage of the project is to show that this should not be a cause of regret, for the minimal state is 'inspiring' as well as right.

In Chapter 1, I shall present an overview of Nozick's libertarianism, while the view of rights sustaining that theory is examined and elaborated in Chapter 2. Here I have tried to be more systematic than Nozick himself, by attempting to delineate the structure of his view and its possible foundations. Chapter 3 examines Nozick's defence of the minimal state against the anarchist, and Chapter 4 assesses Nozick's theory of justice, which is perhaps the most important element of *Anarchy, State, and Utopia*. It is by means of this theory that Nozick is able to argue that no more than the minimal state is justified. Finally, in Chapter 5 we look at the idea of the minimal state as a 'framework for utopia', and, more generally, at Nozick's place in political philosophy. I hope, by then, to have explained not only the attractions of Nozick's view, but also its limitations.

1

Nozick's Libertarianism

Between Anarchy and the State

'If the individual has the right to govern himself, all external government is tyranny'.[1] The case against the state has rarely been put so trenchantly as by Benjamin Tucker, the nineteenth-century American anarchist. So seriously does Nozick take arguments of this type that much of *Anarchy, State, and Utopia* is an attempt to show that, despite the plausibility of the anarchist's case, a state can exist without violating rights.

Nozick, like Tucker, conceives of political philosophy as starting from the premiss that: 'Individuals have rights, and there are things no person or group may do to them (without violating their rights)' (ix). But, unlike Tucker, Nozick argues that anarchism is not the inevitable consequence. His project is to defend the different conclusion that 'a minimal state, limited to the narrow functions of protection against force, theft, fraud, enforcement of contracts, and so on, is justified', but 'any more extensive state will violate persons' rights not to be forced to do certain things' (ix).

Few actual states resemble Nozick's ideal. Some 'welfare states', for example, have programmes for the alleviation of poverty, financed by taxation of the better off. This, Nozick argues, goes beyond the proper, narrow functions of the minimal state, for in redistributing property the state is not protecting, but violating, the rights of individuals. The welfare state forces people to pay their taxes on pain of punishment, and thereby, in Nozick's view, interferes with the rights of those taxed to do as they choose with their own property. The minimal state, on the other hand, has no function but to safeguard property rights.

We can see that in defending the minimal state Nozick has set himself against two quite different types of opponent: the anarchist and the defender of the extensive state. Anarchists attack Nozick's 'statism', and the 'statists' his (near) anarchism. Part of the purpose of this book is to investigate how far Nozick's attempt to secure this midway point – the minimal state – succeeds against attacks from both sides.

Nozick realizes that his project may be unpopular. 'Many persons will reject our conclusions instantly, knowing they don't *want* to believe anything so apparently callous towards the needs and suffering of others' (ix). But Nozick is undaunted, arguing vigorously in defence of what has become known as his 'libertarianism'. Key elements of this defence are Nozick's account of individual rights and his theory of justice, from which he is able to build up a vision of the minimal state. Towards the end of this chapter we shall investigate what life would be like in a libertarian society; would it be as callous as Nozick's critics suppose? First we should take a preliminary look at Nozick's view of rights and justice.

The Thesis of Self-Ownership

We all lead separate lives. We have separate existences. Nozick takes these truisms very seriously and from them he draws a moral conclusion. It is wrong, he argues, to sacrifice one person for the sake of another. One person must not be used as a resource for another. Of course, if I want to sacrifice *myself* then that, perhaps, is to be applauded, but we must not, says Nozick, force someone to suffer some sort of loss or disadvantage just so another may gain. To do so is to ignore the 'separateness of persons'.[2] This is one way of presenting the thesis of self-ownership: the view that only you have the right to decide what is to happen to your life, your liberty and your body, for they belong to no one but you. This thesis looks very plausible and sceptics can often be silenced by reflecting on examples such as that of the 'eye lottery'. Suppose that transplant technology reaches such a pitch of perfection that it becomes possible to transplant eyeballs with a one hundred per cent chance of success. Anyone's eyes may be transplanted into anyone else, without complications. As some people are born with defective eyes, or with no eyes at all, should we redistribute eyes? That is, should we take one eye from some people with two healthy eyes, and give eyes to the blind? Of course, some people may volunteer their eyes for transplant. But what if there were not enough volunteers? Should we have a national lottery, and force the losers to donate an eye?[3] To many this seems monstrous. It would be a better world, of course, if everyone could see, but does this justify holding the eyeball lottery and redistributing eyes?

According to the thesis of self-ownership each of us is the rightful owner of our own body. If we make redistribution of eyes compulsory then we ignore this right, or, as Nozick would say, we violate it, sacrificing one person for the sake of another, and this must not be allowed to happen. Many people, on reflection, would accept that our body rights are absolute in this sense, and would happily draw similar conclusions for the right to life: no one may take my life just to save another, unless I consent. And self-ownership also has consequences for liberty: what I do is my business, and I can do whatever I like, provided I respect the rights of others.

It is important to realize the role played here by consent. Nozick's key idea is that except for purposes of punishment or self-defence the only things others may do to me are those to which I agree. Things which are done to me without my consent are illegitimate, and they violate my rights. Each individual is 'surrounded' by a 'protected sphere' of rights,[4] with which no one may interfere. Nozick maintains that it is by recognizing an individual's rights to non-interference – the right to be left alone – that we respect the separateness of persons.

Nozick is not the first to formulate such a view of rights, and it is sometimes said that the idea of self-ownership stands at the heart of all liberalism.[5] Arguably, it can be found in various forms in Locke, Kant, and Mill. Nozick is distinctive in the emphasis he puts upon rights of self-ownership. As we shall see in the next chapter, they are absolute and override all considerations of need, desert, or happiness. Individual rights, for Nozick, fill the whole political landscape.[6]

The Entitlement Theory of Justice

This view of individual rights to life and liberty accords well with the anarchist intuition that each person has the right of self-government, but some of those initially attracted to Nozick's book by its title, in the hope that they will find a defence of anarchism, may be puzzled by what they read. The anarchism of writers such as Bakunin, Kropotkin, and Proudhon is a romantic, radical theory, which promises a sort of communism without the state. Two features of Nozick's view show that this is not what he will be arguing for: first, that he allows a minimal state, and second the emphasis he places upon private property rights.

It was Proudhon who declared 'Property is theft'. Nozick clearly does not share this opinion, claiming that along with rights to life and to liberty, people can come to have rights to property. These rights too will fall within an individual's 'protected sphere', and where you have a justified right to property, according to Nozick, your right to this property is just as comprehensive and inviolable as your right to your eyes. No one may interfere with your property without your consent, even for the sake of a greater good.

But when do people have rights to property? On what basis, if any, is ownership of private property morally justified? Some people think that property should be distributed on the basis of need, while others believe that it should be allocated only to those who deserve it. Nozick has a different idea. Considerations of entitlement, not desert nor need, should be decisive. But what is entitlement? Suppose someone who is already extremely rich is quite unexpectedly left a further fortune. Certainly we would say that he does not need this extra money, and it may also be that he has done nothing to deserve or merit it. Yet we are inclined to say it is still rightfully his, he is entitled to it, even if he does not need it or deserve it. It is this idea of entitlement upon which Nozick fastens. In effect, he argues that what should be decisive in the question of the justice of a person's property holdings are not features of that person – their needs or merit – but facts about how they obtained the property; did they acquire it in a way that entitles them to it?

There are two basic processes, according to Nozick, by which people may come to be entitled to property. Property may either be justly acquired from those who already justly hold it, or, in certain circumstances, it can be 'appropriated' from nature, if it is unowned. Thus Nozick supplies principles of 'justice in transfer' and 'justice in acquisition' to tell us which methods or procedures must be followed if possession is to be construed as legitimate ownership, rather than, say, theft. A third principle of 'justice in rectification', to remedy any past injustices, completes Nozick's 'entitlement theory of justice'. This theory provides the background to the claim that individuals have absolute private property rights that are just as strong as their body rights.

The Minimal State

According to Nozick, then, we each have absolute rights to life and liberty, and are also able to form absolute rights to property. But the mere fact that we have rights does not guarantee that they are always going to be respected. How can we protect ourselves against those prepared to violate our rights? In present societies we have institutions to protect ourselves. We may call the police, or take those who violate our rights to court. But in an anarchist society, clearly, these courses of action are not available. If there is no state, then, it seems, there are no police or judicial systems. Some idealistic anarchists believe that the state is the root of all evil, and so without the state no one would wish to interfere with the rights of others. Not surprisingly, Nozick does not rely on this view.

Instead Nozick endorses the minimal state, or what has sometimes been called the 'nightwatchman state'. The state is justified, thinks Nozick, only in so far as it protects people against force, fraud, and theft, and enforces contracts. Thus it exists to safeguard rights and this is its sole justification. The state violates rights if it undertakes any more extensive programmes.

It is hard to understand what is so special or unusual about this conception of the just state until we contrast it with the type of government to which we are more accustomed. A modern government has many areas of activity to which it apportions its taxation-funded budget. Thus we find departments of defence, education, health, police, transport, welfare, and so on. We are used to seeing these activities simply as different branches of government. Yet from the libertarian point of view, there are fundamental distinctions to be drawn.

First, there are those branches of government concerned with defending citizens against acts of aggression: the department of defence protects citizens from the actions of foreign invaders, while the police and law courts protect citizens from each other. Second, some sectors of government set out to provide public services of various sorts – roads, fire services, libraries – with the intention of improving the quality of life for everyone. Third, there are areas of government activity to take care of citizens who for some reason – ill health, poverty, unemployment – are unable to take care of themselves. Finally the government may also undertake to supervise individual lives to some extent. In most countries there is some form of censorship (notably censorship of films); in many, certain drugs are prohibited; and in almost all there is some compulsory education. These are areas in which the government forces people to do, or not to do, things apparently for their own good.

Note that only the first of these four sectors concerns the defence of people's rights to non-interference. The second sector goes beyond this, in that it seeks to supply goods and services from which everyone will benefit; the third supplies goods and services from which only part of society will benefit, generally at the expense of those who will not; and the fourth supplies or prohibits goods to all, whether or not they agree.

The minimal state may raise taxes only to cover the first of these sectors – to defend rights to person and property. Nozick argues that the minimal state 'may not use its coercive apparatus for the purpose of getting some citizens to aid others or in order to prohibit activities to people for their *own* good or protection' (ix), so he rules as illegitimate both the third and fourth sectors. We should add on Nozick's behalf, a prohibition of the second sector. The government may not force people to contribute to projects that further their own well-being. Thus we have a bar on compulsory redistribution, and also on all forms of paternalism. Compulsory redistribution is ruled out by Nozick's entitlement theory of justice, which says that transfers are morally justified only if they are entirely voluntary, while paternalism violates an individual's right to the liberty to determine the course of his or her own life. The most startling consequence of Nozick's claims is that the state has no business helping those in poverty: people do not have rights to welfare assistance.

A Framework for Utopia?

It is not easy to imagine what life would be like were government activity pared down in this way. Will we see the poor starve for lack of rights to food? Would houses burn down for want of a fire service? And would there be no roads, no drains, and no electricity supply? Nozick, in fact, claims that the minimal state is 'inspiring as well as right' (ix). Whether the minimal state is *right* is the question pursued throughout this book, but we might now ask, in the light of these questions, why should anyone think that the minimal state is inspiring?

First of all, it is vital to appreciate that although Nozick argues that we may not force the rich to part with their surplus wealth, he certainly does not recommend that they ignore the plight of the poor. He does not seek to discourage private philanthropy. A libertarian may even go so far as to say that it is immoral for the rich to let the poor starve if they are in a position to do anything about it: the rich ought to engage in private redistribution schemes. But it is essential to make the distinction between the morally right and what it is right to enforce by law. It may be wrong not to give to charity, but, for a libertarian, this is no reason to force someone to contribute. Property rights trump duties of benevolence.

The distinction between the morally right and the rightfully enforceable is one we commonly make in other cases. It may be absolutely wrong and morally unforgivable for me to cross the road rather than go to the aid of a fellow citizen lying prostrate on the pavement ahead, but we might be unhappy with the thought that it should be illegal for me to make this immoral choice. Libertarians point out that taxation for redistributive purposes in effect does make it illegal not to contribute to alleviating the plight of the badly off. But it is quite consistent to believe that morally one should aid the poor and the sick, and yet that one should not be forced to do this. And voluntary contributions, in principle, can do more than help the needy. Just as one might provide food for the starving, one might donate resources for a library or museum, and even, perhaps, a road system. That is, charity may fund public goods as well as welfare programmes.

But if all aid were voluntary, how much would be forthcoming? Would the minimal state stimulate or dampen philanthropy? This is, of course, a speculative question, but there are those who argue that current philanthropic activity is much curtailed by the welfare state and the taxation required to sustain it. Abolish the welfare state, reduce tax burdens, and the springs of philanthropy will once more flow. Once more, because, as Milton and Rose Friedman point out, the great age of philanthropy preceded the age of the extensive government: privately financed schools and colleges, foreign missionary activity, non-profit private hospitals, and orphanages, the Salvation Army and the YMCA all date from the nineteenth century.[7] In response it could be urged that the modern pressure for the welfare state was a consequence of the ineffectiveness of nineteenth-century philanthropy. But in any case whether such activity would resume in a new minimal state has, of course, to remain a matter of conjecture.

However, philanthropy is not the only approach to misfortune and the provision of public goods in the minimal state. The free market has some of its own well-known solutions. Those worried about falling sick, or becoming unemployed, may take out insurance to reduce their vulnerability. It is important not to underestimate the potential of the insurance market to protect individuals from whatever contingencies they choose to insure against. But it is just as important not to overestimate this potential. Some are born poor, or sick, and so are not an acceptable risk to an insurance company. It may be hard to renew cover for those suffering from incurable or lengthy ailments. And for those in financial difficulties insurance payments are often the first 'non-essential' expenditure to be sacrificed. None the less, the possibility of insurance reduces one's reliance on the benevolence of others, and would provide a safety net for many in the minimal state, although not for all.

Equally, certain public goods could be provided by individuals or voluntary associations seeking to profit from non-members. Perhaps no one would set up a fountain in the market-place for the free use of all, but the private supply of water, for example, is often economically feasible through piped or bottled provision. A great many goods could be supplied privately for commercial reasons. Other goods, however, might be more difficult to deal with in this way. Some goods are public by nature, in that there is no practical way of preventing those who do not pay their share from enjoying the benefit. Street lighting is one commonly cited example. Goods of this sort may be in short supply in the minimal state.

So far, we have some reasons for thinking that the minimal state would not be as bleak as it first appeared, in that it might well be able to provide a more or less effective substitute for some of the functions of a more extensive state. But clearly little we have seen so far entitles us to the judgement that the minimal state is *inspiring*. So why does Nozick claim this? The answer is that he believes it provides a 'framework for utopia'.

Utopian fantasies are attractive to many, and some of our most imaginative thinkers have spent a great deal of energy designing model societies in which, in their opinion, human life could be lived to the fullest extent.[8] Nozick points out that often a utopian thinker will suppose that he or she is the first truly to understand the nature of the good life for a human being, and so, with this discovery, for the first time a society fully worthy of human beings has become possible. Some utopian proposals are based on a return to self-sufficient agricultural communities, others upon civic societies, but in general, within a single vision only one style of life will be on offer, albeit with a certain permissible range of variation. Such a life expresses, for the thinker, the nature of the fully human life: the good life for human beings.

But Nozick does not agree that there is such a thing as the single good life for human beings. Each individual may have his or her own conception of the good, and it is unlikely that all human beings could live a happy or fulfilling life in one utopian society. To concentrate the mind of would-be utopians, Nozick challenges them to design a single society that would be best for 'Wittgenstein, Elizabeth Taylor, Bertrand Russell, Thomas Merton, Yogi Berra, Allen Ginsburg, Harry Wolfson, Thoreau, Casey Stengel, The Lubavitcher Rebbe, Picasso, Moses, Einstein . . . you and your parents' (310).

The idea behind 'a framework for utopia' is to provide a description of a background against which it is possible to design and live one's own utopia. In the minimal state one group could create a communist village in which all resources are shared, whilst another group creates a perfectionist society in which all comforts are sacrified in the pursuit of high culture. A third group may try to set up a model free market society, and so on. In the minimal state, then, individuals may voluntarily create sub-states of various sorts. There need be no argument about whether society should be organized on capitalist or on socialist lines. Those who favour capitalism can live in a capitalist state, those who favour socialism can live in a socialist state.

It is not easy to see how a more extensive state could provide such a neutral 'framework for utopia'. Those, for example, who wish to live in a certain style of rugged self-sufficiency, like the Amish farmers of Pennsylvania, may find that taxation to supply goods for which they have no desire makes it impossible to meet their financial obligations without working for others. Thus the more extensive one's obligations to the state, the less feasible certain life-styles become. Equally, a non-minimal state may decide to prohibit certain social, sexual, or economic practices and thereby rule out styles of life thought desirable by some of its citizens.

Thus a non-minimal state, it appears, will rule out the possibility of living in certain sorts of communities. Of course, even in the minimal state it may be hard to find enough other people who have the inclination and resources to live out a particular utopian fantasy. But although it may be hard, it is unlikely to be illegal or ruled out by one's obligations to the state, as it may be in a non-minimal state. Certainly questions can be raised about the feasibility and stability of this pluralist utopia, and these will be examined in Chapter 5, but the framework for utopia should be remembered by those convinced of the stark heartlessness of the libertarian vision.

2

Libertarian Rights

Individual Rights vs Utility

Benjamin Tucker, we saw, argued that no state can be morally justified. Nozick replies that a morally legitimate state could exist. The common assumption goes strongly against Tucker, for it seems generally to be thought that the legitimacy of the state is something that needs no argument. It is obvious that some form of state is inevitable, there being no serious alternative, and so this is a sufficient justification for its existence should it be called into question. Nozick disagrees. We must, he feels, *demonstrate* that the state is justified, and this means refuting the anarchist (and, for Nozick, refuting the anarchist without opening the door to the extensive state). But before we take pains to refute the anarchist we should examine whether the anarchist has a case worth answering. Are the assumptions which generate the anarchist's conclusions worth taking seriously? Nozick, however, must take these assumptions very seriously indeed, for they are the same as his own. So for Nozick the anarchist presents a case urgently in need of an answer, and the refutation will consist of showing that those shared assumptions do not, finally, entail the illegitimacy of all forms of the state.

While there are many different arguments for anarchy,[1] Nozick's concern is with the 'individualist anarchist' who reasons from the premises of self-ownership and the separateness of persons encountered in Chapter 1. The individualist anarchist argues that once we examine the consequences of these doctrines, we shall see that all forms of the state are immoral. But not all political philosophers give such emphasis to self-ownership. Utilitarians, for example, might argue from Bentham's premiss that 'each is to count for one and nobody for more than one', or assert, with Sidgwick, that 'the good of any one individual is of no more importance, from the point of view ... of the Universe, than the good of any other.'[2] Either of these premisses, when combined with others, might stand as a foundation for the utilitarian conclusion that we should maximize the total sum of happiness or pleasure in the world, irrespective of how that happiness is distributed. This often intuitively appealing doctrine has radical consequences. It may be that Albert, who has only a bicycle, will get more pleasure from Priscilla's Renault than she does herself, because having the Jaguar and the Volvo she so rarely finds herself using it. So our utilitarian would advocate taking the Renault from Priscilla and giving it to Albert, as this would increase the sum of pleasure in the world. More sophisticated utilitarians may hesitate before drawing this conclusion,[3] but by contrasting Nozick's view with 'crude utilitarianism' we bring Nozick's own position into clearer perspective. Our crude utilitarian is concerned only with maximizing total happiness, whatever means it takes to achieve that goal. Thus the separateness of persons is given no weight at all.

As far as Nozick is concerned, by ignoring the separateness of persons the utilitarian point of view falls into moral error and, Nozick argues, this moral error is associated with a metaphysical error. Why should we take the car from Priscilla and give it to Albert? The utilitarian replies: because this way happiness is maximized. But why should we be interested in maximizing happiness? At this point Nozick supposes that the utilitarian may argue by analogy. Putting 10 per cent of your income into a savings scheme would probably cause you a small drop in immediate happiness. But eventually you will be able to buy the car you want, or your ideal holiday home, or secure your old age against financial worries. If you do this it is likely that your sacrifice will be worthwhile; this will be a happier life, all told, than that of instant gratification. So in our own lives we are often prepared to redistribute benefits and burdens to maximize happiness. We accept present burdens for the sake of future gains. The utilitarian suggests that it is morally right to extend this reasoning to society as a whole, imposing burdens on some for the sake of greater benefits to others, and thereby increasing the sum of happiness in the world.

Nozick, however, seeks to resist this analogy. The reason why it is at least rational for me to save now for future gain is that I will be the person who reaps that gain. That is, there is a single agent who bears the burden and receives the benefit and whose total happiness is increased. Thus my future benefits compensate for my present burdens. But when we take the car from Priscilla, and give it to Albert, there is no single person who suffers the pain and gains the pleasure but whose happiness is maximized by the transaction. What happens is that we reduce Priscilla's happiness while increasing Albert's. As Nozick says, 'nothing more' (33). Nozick, then, accuses the utilitarian of making the metaphysical error of supposing that 'society' itself is an entity that 'experiences' pleasures and pains and whose well-being can be maximized. But there is no such entity, only separate individuals, and one person's pleasure cannot 'compensate' for another's pain.

Some utilitarians would deny that such a metaphysics lies behind their view, claiming that although one person's happiness does not strictly compensate for another's pain nevertheless it is a good thing to impose costs on some people for the sake of greater benefits to others.[4] But Nozick would still accuse such utilitarians of making the moral error of failing to respect the separateness of persons. It is wrong, he argues, to use one person as a 'resource' for others, 'sacrificing' one person's well-being for the sake of others, and utilitarianism says that this is what we should do. Nozick, therefore, sets out to provide a moral view that treats the separateness of persons with the importance he believes it to have. At its heart is the idea that there are certain things an individual has an absolute right to control, and considerations of social welfare cannot overrule these rights. Primarily, for Nozick, one has such rights over one's life and liberty, and the general right to form specific rights to property. More fully, one has the right not to be assaulted, attacked, coerced, defrauded, or cheated, and the right to form secure private property rights by going through certain procedures such as exchange, or receipt by gift, and, in certain circumstances, appropriating from nature. Any such rights to property are, for Nozick, in general as strong as your rights to your own body. Nozick recognizes that this last claim is particularly contentious, and so it requires special defence. We will examine Nozick's account of property rights in full in Chapter 4.

Inviolable Rights

The shared ground between Nozick and the individualist anarchist, then, is the claim that we have very strong rights to life, liberty, and property. Nozick's own libertarian theory of rights is rather more fully articulated than that of many anarchists, and our next task is to examine those features of Nozick's theory which allow him to claim that our rights are inviolable, in that they can never be overridden with justification.

First we must observe that to say Nozick believes that we have rights to life, liberty, and property invites a confusion. Suppose that I am dying of starvation and you are the only person with any food to spare. If we believe that I have a right to life, then we might draw the conclusion that I have a right to your food, since that is the only way I will stay alive. But for Nozick this certainly does not follow, and it is important to see why not. To clarify Nozick's position we can distinguish two sorts of rights: negative and positive. If I have a *positive* right to something this entails that a particular person, or in other cases everyone, has a corresponding duty to provide me with that thing, or whatever is necessary to secure it. So if I have a positive right to life then others must provide me with the things necessary to keep me alive. But a *negative* right to life does not have this implication. Rather it is a right to non-interference. It entails not that someone else has a duty to provide me with what I need to live, but rather that they have a duty to forbear from actions which put my life in jeopardy. In other words, negative rights are rights not to be harmed, or 'interfered with', while positive rights are, in general, rights to be assisted in some way. This distinction may not, in fact, be quite as clear as it first appears, for it presupposes that we can always distinguish between harming another and failing to help them. Further, as we shall see later in this chapter, some rights are not obviously either positive or negative. Nevertheless, thinking in terms of this distinction can help us to understand the nature of Nozick's views.

Nozick allows that we can have positive rights. But except in very special cases they exist only as a result of people voluntarily undertaking the obligations that correspond to those rights – for example, by making a contract. If I hire a doctor to keep me alive I acquire positive rights to the doctor's care and attention. But if I make no such contracts, then, according to Nozick, my only rights are negative rights of non-interference. This doctrine provides the content of the image of a protected sphere of rights, which underwrites the separateness of persons. This, then, is the first important feature of our rights, according to Nozick. They are, in general, negative rights to non-interference.

The second essential component of Nozick's doctrine of rights can be brought out by considering the question of whether one person's rights can conflict with those of another. If, unlike Nozick, we assume that people have positive rights, then conflict may be common. One clear case occurred in the last example where I shall starve unless I eat some of your spare food. Now even though your food is spare, it is still your food and you have a right to it. If you are unwilling to hand it over we have a clash between your property right to the food, and my right to it in pursuit of my right to life. One right must give way. We would, perhaps, be inclined to argue that your right to the food should be overridden, although there is no necessity about this, and we may take a different view in different cases.

This conflict of rights resulted from the clash between a positive right to life and a negative right to property. But what is the position if, like Nozick, we believe the only non-contractual rights are negative rights to non-interference? Can conflicts arise? Suppose we all have negative rights to life, liberty, and property, so no one may rightfully be killed, or have their person or property interfered with, and these are the only rights we have. As long as these rights are universally obeyed it seems that there can be no conflicts. However, the position becomes more complicated when someone threatens to violate another's rights. Suppose a terrorist group threatens that unless we hand over to them a judge who has imprisoned a member of their group they will engage in an extensive campaign of terror, killing many and destroying property. We have no reason to doubt that in fact they will do this if we do not comply. What should we do?

We might agree that the judge has a right to life and liberty, at least in the sense that no interference with either can be justified. It is clear that handing over the judge would constitute an interference with her liberty, and would probably lead to her torture and death. To surrender the judge to the terrorists would be to violate her rights to non-interference, so it would seem to follow that we should not do this.

But in reply, it might be said that if we refuse the terrorists' demands then far more extensive violations of rights would result. Many innocent citizens will die or have their property destroyed. And so, if we really care about rights we should deliver the judge to the terrorists, as this will lead to fewer rights violations in the end. Someone who takes this view cannot argue that rights are absolute or inviolable in the sense that they can never justifiably be overridden. For it is plausible that for any possible right there are circumstances in which it may be necessary to violate that particular right in order to minimize long-term rights violations.

Nozick, of course, strongly rejects the argument that we should surrender the judge to the terrorists. Those who want to hand her over advocate what Nozick calls a sort of 'utilitarianism of rights' according to which obedience to rights is a goal to be maximized, just as a classical utilitarian wants to maximize well-being or happiness. Thus they allow that rights may be overridden for the sake of more important or more numerous rights. But Nozick presents an entirely different theory: one which sees rights not only as negative but also as providing 'side constraints' on action. This is the second key feature of Nozick's theory of rights.

On the side-constraint view the rights of individuals should be considered as blocks or constraints on the actions of others. If the judge has a right to liberty then we should not adopt any course of action that violates her right, irrespective of the consequence. The course of action in which we hand over the judge is, morally speaking, closed to us. The question of maximization does not arise, and from the standpoint of morality, there is, according to Nozick, only one thing to do in the case under consideration: refuse the terrorists' demands, whatever the consequences.[5]

Strictly, the doctrine that rights are to be seen as side constraints should be distinguished from the issue of 'dirty hands'. One reason why we might be reluctant to hand over the judge is that if we do, we directly violate someone's rights, whereas if we do not, rights will get violated, but not by us. Thus a desire to keep one's hands 'clean' would lead one to refuse to hand over the judge. For Nozick this instruction to keep your hands clean is part of the doctrine of side constraints, but the side-constraint doctrine has a further aspect. I should not violate rights even to minimize *my own* future violation of rights. Suppose, for example, I am a kleptomaniac whose condition can be controlled only by the use of drugs. If I do not take my medicine today, I will commit many acts of theft tomorrow. Suppose also that I have run out of medicine, and the only accessible supply is owned by you. You refuse to part with any. Should I (non-compulsively) steal some of your medicine today, so that I will not (compulsively) steal a great many other things tomorrow?[6] Nozick's view appears to be that it would be wrong for me to steal your medicine, for my concern should always be to try to avoid violating rights at the present time. Thus we do not precisely have a directive to keep our hands clean, but to keep them as clean as we can *now*, even though that means they will end up dirtier in the future than otherwise they might have done.

To argue that first we have only negative rights and second they are to be seen as side constraints, not goals to be maximized, will not yet ensure that these rights are inviolable. It has also to be shown that no other considerations can override these rights. We have seen that Nozick rejects one purported superior claim: no amount of social utility can 'trump' a right. However other values too can conflict with rights claims and these conflicts must be adjudicated. For example, occasionally the exercise of private property rights comes into conflict with the preservation of the natural environment or of ancient cultural artifacts. Should the owner of a site of special archaeological interest be allowed to demolish or destroy whatever is there? Here we see private property rights clash with other claims, based, not on rights, but perhaps on aesthetic or historical grounds. Nor are these other claims necessarily reducible to those of happiness. Human happiness may be best served by turning the Parthenon into a theme park, yet many would argue that even so it is more important that the Parthenon remain intact. Thus it must be thought to have a value distinct from its contribution to human happiness. So how do we judge disputes between rights and other values?

For Nozick the answer is simple. In so far as we are talking about enforceable obligations – those we may legitimately enforce by sanction of punishment – rights are exhaustive. Our only enforceable moral concerns are based on rights. Thus private property rights, for example, will always take moral priority over considerations of archaeological value. Does this mean that Nozick believes nothing to be of value except rights? Of course not. Nozick agrees that many different things are of varying forms of value. It would be a great pity if property developers built an office block on top of ancient remains. But if the developers legitimately own the site, then they have a perfect right to build on it even if the result is the destruction of something of great value. We have no business preventing the owners from doing what they want to do with their land, although we might rightly be appalled at this action. More recently Nozick has reiterated the distinction between what is right and what is right to enforce, pointing out that there is much more to morality than rights, but that political philosophy is concerned with enforceable obligations and that these are exhausted by rights.[7] Thus the third essential feature of Nozick's theory of rights is that, politically, rights are our only concern: they are exhaustive.

Treating rights as negative, construing them as providing side constraints, and as being exhaustive – trumping all other moral considerations – allows Nozick to insist that rights have a secure, absolute character. They may not be overridden for the sake of public welfare, nor for the sake of other rights, nor indeed for any other reason.[8] Of course rights will in fact be violated by murderers and thieves, just as people's rights would be violated by the terrorists if we did not hand over the judge, but the point is that rights can never be overridden with justification.

Questions, of course, can be raised about each of the three central features of Nozick's rights theory. This is not to say that the theory is, for that reason, false, but to point out that it is just one theory among many, and thus requires argument. Against the view that we have negative rights and only negative rights, the utilitarian may argue that we have no moral rights whatsoever, beyond the right to be 'counted as one' in the utilitarian calculus. An entirely different type of objection to the negative-rights doctrine is raised by certain socialist and liberal egalitarian writers; that we have positive rights to life and a decent standard of living. Against the claim that rights are exhaustive, arguments may be made about other values (such as the preservation of the natural environment) which may override rights in some cases. Finally, we have seen that an alternative to the side-constraint structure of rights is the 'utilitarianism of rights' theory. If any of these objections, or alternative views, can be substantiated then the claim that rights are inviolable fails. We will return to some of these issues later; for the moment we should just remember that Nozick's theory is not obviously true, nor the only theory in the field.

Natural Rights and John Locke

Not only are our rights inviolable, Nozick would argue, they are natural too. H. L. A. Hart points out two important characteristics of a natural right. First, a natural right 'is one which all men have if they are capable of choice: they have it *qua* men and not only if they are members of some society or stand in some special relation to each other.' Second, a natural right 'is not created or conferred by men's voluntary action.'[9] Thus a natural right is not created by law or convention, but exists independently of human action. Indeed part of the point of claiming that humans have natural rights is to provide a standpoint from which one is able to criticize human laws and conventions.

Could there be such things as natural rights? Human beings naturally have arms and legs. Do they just as naturally have rights? Clearly natural rights do not exist in the sense in which biological features of individuals exist. According to Bentham the idea of a natural right is absurd, and self-contradictory. Rights, he claimed, are given by law. The only rights that make sense, then, are legal rights, created by the law of man, and divine rights, if one accepts the existence of a divine law-giver. 'Right with me is the child of law; from different operations of the law result different sorts of rights. A natural right is a son that never had a father.'[10] Consequently 'Natural Rights is simple nonsense: natural and imprescriptible [i.e. inviolable] rights, rhetorical nonsense, – nonsense upon stilts.'[11]

Much as we may admire Bentham's own rhetoric, natural rights seem no more – and no less – metaphysically suspicious than the idea of any universal moral requirement. As Dworkin puts it, to believe in natural rights is simply to take 'the protection of certain individual choices as fundamental'.[12] Indeed, whether we have Nozickian natural rights essentially comes down to two questions. First, do all human beings have the enforceable moral duty to refrain from 'aggressing' on others? Second, are these all the enforceable moral duties human beings have, unless they create others by their voluntary agreement? Nozick, of course, replies in the affirmative to both questions. But what reasons does he have for giving these replies, and what reasons might be suggested on his behalf ?

Earlier I mentioned that Nozick owes a great deal to John

Locke. Often the two writers are taken to converge on their accounts of natural rights, for here Nozick explicitly follows Locke. In order, then, to try to discover the argument for Nozick's theory of rights it is worth paying some attention to Locke's own project in political philosophy and to see how Locke defends his claim that we have natural rights. Why did Locke assert that human beings have natural rights, and what considerations did he marshal to defend this view?

Locke's major work in political philosophy – *Two Treatises of Government* (1690) – was intended as a reply to the writings of Sir Robert Filmer, who had set out to defend the doctrine of the divine right of kings in his work *Patriarcha* (1680). But Locke took the opportunity of going far beyond this negative, critical task by presenting in the *Second Treatise* his own view of the proper foundation and limits of sovereign power. Although it is the *Second Treatise* which has had such influence on Nozick and other modern writers it is worth putting this in context by saying a little about Locke's *First Treatise*.

In *Patriarcha*, Filmer argued that the monarch rules by a divine, absolute right which can be traced back by succession to God's original bestowal of the world upon Adam. The basic argument is a simple one. God created Adam as ruler of the world, with absolute power over the earth and its creatures and over other human beings. Adam has bequeathed this power to his descendants. Any present king or queen has thereby received in succession from Adam the god-given right of absolute rule. Consequently the monarch's rightful power is unlimited, and no considerations of justice can speak against any of his or her deeds. The monarch may rightfully act in an arbitrary fashion, imprisoning or executing enemies or the innocent, and confiscating property, which, after all, ultimately belongs to the monarch anyway.

Locke set out to provide a thorough demolition of Filmer's views, attempting to refute him at every turn. First he argues that the scriptures do not support the interpretation that God gave to Adam the right to govern other men. Second, even if Adam was given this right, there is no reason to think that his heirs could inherit his title to legitimate rule (as opposed to his title in property). Third, even if the right to rule could be bequeathed, rules of succession are largely a matter of convention, not laws of God or nature, and so who had the right to succeed could not, in all cases, be determined in a non-arbitrary way. Finally, even if there was a fact about who had the right to succeed, the knowledge of who now has this right is lost, and there is no reason to think that the present monarch is the rightful ruler appointed by God in succession from Adam.

Locke's positive views, expounded in the *Second Treatise*, begin with the argument that biblical authority does not support Filmer's position but requires a quite different interpretation. He claims that the scriptures, when properly read, reveal that God did not give the earth to Adam as sole owner, but on behalf of all human beings, who own the earth in common. God created human beings free, equal, and independent[13] with no natural superiors on earth and thus not subject to the rule of any other person.

But if it is true that, as Rousseau was later to say, man is 'born free', we must ask to what do we owe the existence of the state, and our apparent obligation to obey its dictates? We will take up this question in the next chapter, but first we must examine what Locke means by saying that human beings are naturally free, equal, and independent. That is, what would life be like according to Locke, without the state, in a 'state of nature' where all are free and may 'dispose of their Possessions and persons as they think fit ... without asking leave, or depending on the Will of any other Man'?[14]

Locke suggests that 'though this be a State of Liberty, yet it is not a State of Licence'.[15] Even in the state of nature there are limits to what people may legitimately do, even though they are equal and independent. These limits are given by the Law of Nature which, Locke says, is also a law of reason, and, the law of God. The Law of Nature tells us that we are God's property, sent into the world by God, and 'made to last during his ... pleasure'. Accordingly 'no-one ought to harm another in his Life, Health, Liberty or Possession.' In essence, mankind is to be preserved as much as possible, but subject to this constraint humans in the state of nature may do as they 'think fit'.

It follows that human beings should respect the life and liberty of each other, and therefore Locke argues that the law of nature grants rights to life and liberty; that is, he claims we have natural rights. Locke goes on to argue that, from this foundation, there would also be private property rights in the state of nature. We will look further into this in Chapter 4, but the present point is to recognize that Locke argued for natural rights to 'Life, Liberty and Estate', a view with clear affinities to that of Nozick.

We are looking for a foundation for Nozickian natural rights – a reason to believe we have those rights Nozick claims we have. Can Nozick gain any support from Locke's view, which partially inspired his own? Brief reflection shows that this is highly unlikely. We saw that, in arguing against Filmer, Locke did not argue, as many modern philosophers might, that theology has no place in political philosophy. Instead he argued that a proper understanding of the scriptures reveals to us that man is to be preserved as much as possible, and it was from this that he derived his account of natural rights. There are two reasons why Nozick cannot take over this view of the foundation of rights. First, Nozick would not be willing to rest the case for his theory on biblical authority. Second, and more important, if the foundation of the theory of rights is the general preservation of mankind then the content of these rights cannot be Nozickian. For, first, preservation rights would, in some cases, generate positive rights to survive; the starving have a right to aid from those with surplus, as Locke admits in the *First Treatise*.[16] Second, having a maximizing principle of 'preservation as much as possible' it appears that Locke ought to endorse a 'utilitarianism of rights' view, not a side-constraint view. So Nozick cannot claim a Lockean foundation for his view of natural rights.

Kantian Foundations and the Meaning of Life

If there is no Lockean foundation for Nozick's theory of rights, what, then, is its foundation? In *Anarchy, State, and Utopia* this question, surprisingly, is barely addressed, even though Nozick recognizes the undesirability of failing to provide a 'completely accurate statement of the moral background including the precise statement of the moral theory and its underlying basis.' Thus he writes, perhaps unfairly to Locke,

> That task is so crucial, the gap left without its accomplishment so yawning, that it is only a minor comfort to note that we here are following the respectable tradition of Locke, who does not provide anything remotely resembling a satisfactory explanation of the status and basis of the law of nature in his *Second Treatise*. (9)

Yet Nozick is not entirely silent. There are various hints that a partly Kantian inspiration lurks behind his view, and it seems Nozick believes that his theory is Kantian in flavour, if not through and through. In fact, Nozick takes over and adapts just one Kantian idea, an idea generally referred to as the 'Second Formulation of the Categorical Imperative': 'Act in such a way that you always treat humanity ... never simply as a means, but always at the same time as an end.'[17] Thus Nozick argues that 'Side constraints upon action reflect the underlying Kantian principle that individuals are ends and not merely means' (30–1). Here, then, is the prospect of an argument to defend Nozick's account of natural rights.

It is reasonably clear what is meant by talking of using a person merely as a means. This is often elucidated by the further metaphor of treating someone as a tool or instrument, using someone only with regard to your own ends, as you might use a hammer, umbrella, or a doormat. Aristotle referred to slaves as 'living instruments'. If I am accused of treating another *merely* as a means, this is generally taken to imply that in my action towards the other person there is something about that person I am overlooking, neglecting, or disregarding; something which makes treating them purely as an instrument to my own purposes – using them – wholly inappropriate. To treat people as ends in themselves is to act towards them in a way which respects this characteristic.

What characteristic do humans possess which makes it wrong to treat them as means? For Kant the possession of a rational will is central. Human beings are capable of making rational choices, of agreeing and disagreeing with suggested courses of action which affect them, and this marks the difference between persons and instruments. Thus in Kant's view to treat another as an end is to respect their rational will.

In *Anarchy, State,* and *Utopia* Nozick presents his own view of the reason why it is inappropriate to treat people as means, a view with clear Kantian affinities. Starting from the observation that many thinkers have focused on the traits of rationality, free will, and moral agency, Nozick notes that no one of these features is sufficient to show that its possessor deserves special treatment. Just because, for example, a being has free will, why is *that* a reason to allow it to act freely? Nozick's more complex proposal lights upon the further feature of 'the ability to regulate and guide its life in accordance with some overall conception it chooses to accept' (49).

This, when added to the aforementioned traits of rationality, free will, and moral agency, presents a picture of

> something whose significance is clear: a being able to formulate long-term plans for its life, able to consider and decide on the basis of abstract principles or considerations it formulates to itself and hence not merely the plaything of immediate stimuli, a being that limits its own behaviour in accordance with some principles or picture it has of what an appropriate life is for itself and others, and so on. (49)

The significance of this picture is, Nozick conjectures, 'connected with that elusive and difficult notion: the meaning of life' (50). Thus people are to be treated as ends, not merely means, because they are capable of lives with meaning. There is certainly something attractive about this proposal, but how can it function as a defence of libertarian rights? Nozick does not explicitly say. However, one idea is that, first, the meaningful life is what we can call the 'self-shaping' life, and second, to live the self-shaping life, libertarian rights are, in some way, appropriate. It is not clear whether Nozick would wish to claim that it is only possible to shape one's life if one possesses the libertarian rights, or, less strongly, the best chance one has to shape one's life is to have the libertarian rights. Nevertheless, whichever view is endorsed we have a promising sketch of a connection between libertarian rights and the meaningful life, and if the premises are defensible then the result is important and exciting.

How acceptable is Nozick's sketch of the conditions of a meaningful life? It is plausible that Nozick has captured part of what it is to lead a life with meaning. I say 'part' because many would think Nozick has left out one element of immense importance: attachments to others. This involves seeing oneself as part of a network of differing human relations based on mutual affection and mutual support. Even further removed from Nozick's conception is the idea that a fully human life is one which is, at least in part, lived *for* others.[18] If either of these features were thought central then an entirely different view of rights might well spring forth – one involving duties to aid others as well as the right to receive aid. Or indeed it might be concluded that taking the concept of 'right' as fundamental in political philosophy is mis-

taken, and that political philosophy should build on the concept of
'human social nature'. However, let us restrict our investigation to
Nozick's own conception of the meaning of life to see whether, on
the basis of that conception, libertarian rights can be defended.

To make his defence, Nozick must complete two tasks. First he
must show that the self-shaping life requires rights to non-
interference. Second, he must show that such a life requires these
to be inviolable, and, in particular, that it *rules out* enforceable
duties to aid other people – positive rights. To defend rights of
non-interference, Nozick might call upon Hobbes as a powerful
ally.[19] In a state of nature, with no enforceable rights or duties at all

> there is no place for Industry; because the fruit thereof is uncertain:
> and consequently no Culture of the Earth; no Navigation or use of
> the commodities that may be imported by sea; no commodious
> Building; no Instruments of moving, and removing such things as
> require much force; no Knowledge of the face of the earth; no
> account of Time; no Arts; no Letters; no Society; and which is
> worst of all, continuall feare, and danger of violent death; And the
> life of man, solitary, poore, nasty, brutish, and short.[20]

If Hobbes had been of a different philosophical temperament he
might well have ended this passage by observing that in such
conditions, life has no meaning.

It may be more difficult to show that the best chance of living a
self-shaping life demands specifically the Nozickian catalogue of
negative rights, and no more. However, the thought that the best
sort of valuable life can only be lived if one possesses libertarian
rights is not without some initial plausibility. Ayn Rand, a highly
vocal, although philosophically less sophisticated, precursor of
Nozick and libertarianism, energetically presented this view in her
various writings.[21]

Rand's view appears to be that there is a particular type of life
which is most rational, most free, and most valuable in itself. This
is the life of being 'true to one's self' and incorporates having the
courage to follow one's vision, taking control of, and full responsibility for, one's life. Thus the life of value also involves not being
the 'slave' of others, not pandering to the demands of the public,
nor being constrained by the false wisdom of ages. The key claim
must be that unless one is granted absolute rights to non-
interference and, most importantly, freedom from the claims of

others, it is likely that this life will not be available, or at least it cannot be guaranteed that this life will be available. Thus, to ensure people the possibility of meaningful lives, it is necessary to grant them the libertarian rights.

Nozick has somewhat disassociated himself from Rand's position[22] and would not endorse every aspect of this picture. Certainly there are some potentially worrying anti-liberal features here, such as the claim that a particular form of life is best or most valuable. This difficult issue will be discussed more fully in Chapter 5, in the context of Nozick's utopianism and its relation to liberalism. For the moment the point is simply to present a sketch of one way of making out the connection between libertarian rights and the ability to shape one's own life, and thus between libertarian rights and Nozick's conception of the meaning of life.

Is it true that giving people libertarian rights is the best way to give them the opportunity to shape their own lives? On Nozick's own conception of the meaning of life, does granting libertarian rights best advance people's opportunity to live meaningful lives? The problem with this is that, if people have only negative rights, then there is no guarantee that many individuals will, in fact, be in a position to lead lives worth living. Perhaps in such a society many people will have to endure unrelieved poverty. Some may starve, and others lead menial lives. In other words, the cost of creating a world in which talented people, with luck on their side, live a life of great meaning, might be that a significant section of the population can do little better than strive to secure their day-to-day survival.

With this in mind Samuel Scheffler has suggested a different theory of rights which, he claims, fits better with a concern for 'the meaningful life':

> Every person has a natural right to a sufficient share of every distributable good whose enjoyment is a necessary condition of the person's having a reasonable chance of living a decent and fulfilling life, subject only to the following qualification. No person has a natural right to any good which can only be obtained by preventing someone else from having a reasonable chance of living a decent and fulfilling life.[23]

It would seem to follow from this that each person has 'a right to adequate food, clothing, shelter, and medical care',[24] provided that this does not require taking such things away from others who also need them. Scheffler's point might be made by observing that one necessary condition of leading a meaningful life is to lead a life. So if we really are concerned to ensure that people have meaningful lives we should, at the very least, grant them those things necessary to stay alive. Thus people should have positive rights to food, shelter, and so forth.

What could Nozick or Rand say to Scheffler? The immediate objection must be that if we allow positive rights, this means positive duties, and this means that people will have enforceable moral claims to assistance from each other. If it is true that the most meaningful life requires peace and security from the claims of others, as Rand implies, then if we grant positive welfare rights the most meaningful life becomes unavailable. Everyone will have to spend part of his or her time on charitable work. But how plausible is this reply? Might not obligations be met simply by paying taxes? To consider this issue further would be to anticipate the discussion of Nozick's striking claim that 'taxation is forced labour' which I shall discuss in Chapter 4. Let us, for the moment, assume that if we grant welfare rights to all then it will become either impossible or extremely difficult for anyone to lead the most meaningful life, according to Nozick's conception of the meaningful life.

Where does this leave us? We asked whether it was true that granting libertarian rights gives people the best opportunity to shape their lives and, thereby, live meaningful lives. It can now be seen that there is a sense in which this question is not well formed, for it glosses over an ambiguity. By 'best opportunity to lead a meaningful life' do we mean '*best chance* of leading a meaningful life', or do we mean 'chance of living the *most meaningful* life'? Rand and Nozick maintain that the most meaningful life can only be lived with libertarian rights. Scheffler counters that to have the best chance of living a meaningful life we need welfare rights. The examples so far show that both sides might be correct; it is possible to agree with both, and assert that, while to have a chance of living the most meaningful life it is necessary to be granted libertarian rights, the possession of welfare rights gives the best prospect of living some sort of meaningful life. The lesson is that the project of giving people the best opportunity to lead meaningful lives appears not to determine a single theory of rights.

Although Nozick does not take the discussion this far, his best strategy might be to go onto the attack. If it can be shown that the provision of welfare rights would, rather than giving people the opportunity to live meaningful lives, take that possibility away, then the problem is solved in Nozick's favour. For example, it might be argued that giving people positive rights to aid is to treat them like children, or to infantilize them. Worse, it creates a dependency culture in which, far from shaping their own lives, people depend on others even for their day-to-day needs. Thus to give people the 'security' of positive rights is also to take away any chance they may have of leading a meaningful life. So, if this can be sustained, Scheffler's case is self-defeating.

I cannot take this matter any further here. Certainly great care is required to make sure that good points are neither exaggerated nor ignored if this debate is to be settled. My purpose has been to investigate how well Nozick is able to defend his theory of natural rights. To conclude this discussion, let me draw attention to those points where Nozick's argument is incomplete. First, his conception of the meaningful life is not uncontroversial, and a different conception may lead to an entirely different theory of rights, or to a political theory in which some other concept is taken as fundamental. Second, even on Nozick's own conception of a meaningful life it is far from clear that Nozick's theory of rights is to be preferred to Scheffler's. Nozick has not established his case. But he is under no illusions about this, and in *Anarchy, State, and Utopia* he marks the problem down as an area for future research. Nozick's most relevant subsequent research appears in his *Philosophical Explanations*. Although there Nozick somewhat deepens his conception of a meaningful life, little he says goes any way to settling the problems just raised.

Self-Defence and Punishment

Let us now leave aside the question of the ultimate justification of Nozick's theory of rights, and turn our attention to its further elaboration. In particular, if we have rights to non-interference must it follow that aggression and violence will always be morally prohibited? Here again Nozick takes his lead from Locke. Locke's position, in essence, is that although it is never legitimate to initiate force, there are, nevertheless, occasions on which force is the morally appropriate response to force or threats of force. The most obvious suggestion is that we have a natural right of self-defence. Nozick agrees that individuals may legitimately defend themselves against would-be invaders of rights. Locke even argues that there are circumstances in which it can be lawful 'for a man to kill a thief'.[25] He argues that if someone threatens my property I have no good reason to suppose that he or she would not also take my liberty or my life. In this sense, then, a thief threatens to destroy me, and since as Locke claims 'I should have a right to destroy that which threatens me with destruction', I may rightfully kill the thief.

Nozick makes no comment on this argument. Certainly he would not endorse its application to every case of theft, but then, one hopes, neither would Locke. Nozick, rather, argues that self-defence should be proportional to the harm threatened, although the self-defender may also 'draw' on the rightful punishment. This brings us to a second category of acceptable force. Nozick follows Locke in claiming that it is legitimate for individuals to punish those who violate their rights. Locke's view is that the law of nature tells us that although we may punish a criminal, one may not 'use a Criminal according to the passionate heats, or boundless extravagance of his will, but only to retribute to him, so far as calm reason and conscience dictate, what is proportionate to his transgression, which is so much as may serve for Reparation and Restraint.'[26] Thus, in addition to the right to self-defence, we also have a right to punish.

Whether we should classify these rights to self-defence and to punish offenders as negative rights is hard to decide. On the one hand, rights to punish and defend oneself are not rights to non-interference. On the other hand, they are not, in themselves, rights to aid or assistance either. Thus the distinction that helped us to understand Nozick's theory may well break down here. We shall see in the next chapter the consequences of this for Nozick's defence of the state.

Going beyond Locke, Nozick opens discussion on two further areas of possibly legitimate force: 'innocent threats', and 'innocent shields of threats'. Nozick asks 'If someone picks up a third party and throws him at you down at the bottom of a deep well . . . Even though the falling person would survive his fall onto you, may you use your ray gun to disintegrate the falling body before it crushes and kills you?' (34). May you, in other words, kill an innocent person who, through no fault of their own, threatens your life?

Similar examples can be concocted in which the only way of saving your life involves killing an innocent third party who is, unwittingly or unwillingly, shielding the person who threatens your life. Nozick wants to argue that at least in the case of innocent threats, force may sometimes be legitimate, but, he adds, 'I tiptoe around these incredibly difficult issues here, merely noting that a view that says it makes nonaggression central must resolve them explictly at some point' (35).

To summarize Nozick's view of libertarian rights, he argues that all human beings have rights to life and liberty, and can also form equally strong rights to property. Fundamentally our rights underlie the moral prohibition against 'aggression', both to person and property. These rights are said to be inviolable, in that they can never be overridden with justification. This Nozick is able to ensure by claiming that our rights are negative, and that they are to be understood as providing side constraints. This appears to have the consequence that they can never clash with each other. Also rights are, politically speaking, exhaustive, which means that they can never be overridden by any other consideration or value, be it social utility, aesthetic beauty, or whatever. These rights do not rest on human law or convention, and thus are natural, and possessed by all human beings in all forms of society (unless they voluntarily give them up). The foundation, or justification, for libertarian rights is, conjectures Nozick, 'to do with the meaning of life', although Nozick admits that this line of argument amounts to little more than a suggestion. Finally, the picture is elaborated to include rights to self-defence and to punish those who offend against our natural rights.

3

Defending the Minimal State

The Case for Anarchy

Even though Nozick has not firmly established an appropriate line of defence for his view that human beings have natural rights to life and liberty, this view will 'strike a chord' with many. Indeed something like a weaker version of Nozick's doctrine may now seem undeniable if we phrase it Locke's way: human beings are naturally free, equal, and independent, with no natural superiors on earth.

It is worth recalling the context of Locke's claim; it formed part of an attack on Filmer's doctrine of the divine right of kings. If human beings are naturally free, equal and independent, then no king can have a natural or God-given right to rule. But does this mean that no king or sovereign can have any right to rule? Benjamin Tucker looms once more. If the Lockean natural right to liberty is the right to govern oneself, anarchy appears swiftly to follow.

Must sovereign or state govern in a way which threatens self-government? Of course a paternalistic state, directing people's lives and arbitrarily enforcing and prohibiting types of behaviour, restricts liberty in important ways. But a Nozickian minimal state would not do this. It would simply provide a police force, an army, and law courts. Does the existence of these institutions, if they exist only to enforce natural law, constitute a threat to individual liberty? One common anarchist rejoinder is that if such power exists it will inevitably be abused, but this is not Nozick's worry about the state. He has a very different reason for thinking that once you grant people their natural rights, there may be no room for the state.

To appreciate Nozick's concern we must ask, first, what is a state? Nozick, wisely, does not attempt to provide a strict definition, but he endorses the claim of Max Weber and others that 'having a monopoly on the use of force in a geographical area . . . [is] crucial to the existence of a state' (23). Things are not quite as tidy as we might hope, for, as Nozick also points out (he cites Marshall Cohen) states can exist without actually possessing a monopoly on force, as other groups, 'the Mafia, KKK, White Citizens Council, striking unionists, and Weathermen' (23) may also, in fact, use force. Still the state claims exclusive right to authorize and oversee the use of force within its boundaries, and that right will generally be recognized as legitimate. This we can call the first central feature of a state. A second central feature is that, in principle, it offers protection to anyone who resides within its borders. Nozick's strategy is to bring out the apparent conflict between these features of the state and the recognition of natural rights.

On Nozick's account of our rights the very existence of the state would appear to violate those rights. The argument is that any state claims to be the sole legitimate authorizer of force, but no institution can have this right. Each of us, according to the natural-rights tradition, has the right to self-defence and to punish those who violate our rights. Anyone who attempts to prohibit others from exercising these rights is acting illegitimately, so the state is immoral if it claims for itself the monopoly which is so crucial to its existence. Therefore if we recognize Nozickian rights it seems we must reject even the minimal state.

Furthermore, the second central feature of the state – the protection of all – also appears inconsistent with natural rights; surprisingly enough, it appears to conflict with natural rights to property. A state which offers protection to all offers it to rich and to poor, those who can pay and those who cannot afford to. But someone must pay the expenses of the state and its officials. A state, then, must require some people to pay for services provided for other people. It must, that is, engage in compulsory redistribution[1] and this, for Nozick, is a violation of the entitlement theory of justice mentioned in Chapter 1, and to be discussed

in detail in Chapter 4. This is a second argument designed to show
that even the minimal state appears immoral.

The Lockean Predicament

Should we regret the apparent immorality of the state? How good
is life under anarchism? In a Nozickian anarchy, or Lockean state
of nature, we have rights to life, liberty, and property, and the right
to enforce those rights. Yet an obvious thought is that even if, from
a moral point of view, we have those rights in the state of nature, it
is not until they are supported by an institutional framework of
law, and a machinery of law enforcement, that they will be
respected. So, it may be urged, even if we do have these rights,
formally speaking, in anarchy, they will be worthless as we will not
have the power to enjoy them. We will be subject to the constant
fears of murder, enslavement, and theft. This is a familiar argument
against anarchism: it leads to anarchy, in the popular sense of chaos
and violence.

However this is not Locke's objection to the state of nature. He
does, of course, admit that in the state of nature rights violations
would at least be contemplated – why else discuss the theory of
punishment? – but he is careful to distinguish the state of nature
from a Hobbesian state of war of all against all. Locke believed that
in the state of nature rights would generally, although not always,
be respected. People behave, for the most part as they ought.

Now Locke reports ''Tis often asked as a mighty Objection,
where are, or ever were, there any men in such a state of nature?'[2]
We may also be interested in the distinct question: how could we
know what life would be like in the state of nature, even if it did,
once, exist? Part of Locke's answer to the first question also gives
him an answer to the second: the 'World never was, nor never will
be without numbers of Men [in the state of nature].' He claims that
humans lived in the state of nature before they joined together to
make civil societies, and that, in the seventeenth century, much of
America was in this situation. More interestingly, he also argues
that heads of different states are in the state of nature with respect
to each other, if there is no higher body on earth which has
authority over them. Whatever we think of the historical claim,
this latter point suggests that at least some people have been in a
state of nature at some time. The interest of this observation is that

it gives us some idea of what life might be like in a more generalized state of nature: look and see how 'Princes' behave with respect to each other. In fact, Bertrand Russell used exactly this observation as an argument against anarchy. Princes, or at least governments, in the state of nature, he pointed out, led to the First World War, from which he concluded, first, that human beings could not live happily in an anarchic state, and second a single world government was necessary for world peace.[3] Locke, it would seem, had no more reason to be optimistic. During much of Locke's lifetime England was at war of one sort or another. Despite all this, however, he was convinced that the state of nature need not be a state of war.

So if the state of nature is not a state of war, why leave? What possible advantages are there in civil society? Locke's answer is that the problem lies in the administration of justice. It is not that people deliberately set out to violate the rights of others, or even that they act without regard to those rights. Rather, 'every one has the Executive Power of the Law of Nature'. This leads to three problems. First, people might differ in their interpretations of the law of nature. Second, there is no institutional third party to which disputes may be sent for adjudication, so individuals must decide between themselves whether a wrong has been committed, and if so what is a just and fitting punishment. Thus, every person is a judge in his or her own case, and this leaves each case with two judges, each biased in their own favour by 'self-love . . . ill-nature, passion or revenge.' Finally people will often lack the power to enforce any judgement made. Consequently, for Locke there are overwhelming advantages of a legislature to make a stable, publicly knowable, body of law, a judiciary to apply it, and an executive to enforce it. He says 'I easily grant that Civil Government is the proper remedy for the inconveniences of the State of Nature.'[4]

This criticism of the state of nature leaves us with what we can call the 'Lockean predicament'. The theory of rights shows that anarchy is morally required, but considerations based on the difficulties of the administration of justice in anarchy show that a state would be a great improvement. We cannot, it appears, have the state without violating people's natural rights, but our lives would be better if we did have a state. Is there any way out, or does political philosophy necessarily end with 'moral tragedy'?

One suggestion is that the predicament forces us to make a choice between natural rights and the security given by the state.

For many people, if the assumption of natural rights shows that the state is immoral, then so much the worse for natural rights, which must be rejected. For Nozick, however, rejecting or amending the theory of rights is out of the question. The theory of rights is his starting point in political philosophy, his one fixed point. To give up the theory so easily would be to reject his entire project. If natural rights entail anarchy, then, for Nozick, it is anarchy we must have, whatever advantages the state would give us. Nozick's quest is to reconcile the state and natural rights, not to 'justify' the state by abandoning those rights.

We might ask: is the Nozickian project of reconciliation worth carrying out? Those who see either the state or individual natural rights as valueless, will remain unpersuaded, and will even deny that there is a Lockean predicament. Yet it seems that for almost everyone there are moods or moments in which they have great sympathy for the individualist anarchist plea for independence, while at other times they perceive quite clearly the benefits of the state. If so then all of us will have an interest in something like Nozick's project even if, finally, our conclusion is to reject natural rights or the legitimacy of the state.

Consent Theory

Locke, of course, made his own attempt to reconcile autonomy and the state: the theory of consent. In effect, all who enter civil society agree to transfer to the state their rights to punish. The state, then, is able to claim a legitimate monopoly of force, justified by the voluntary transference of individual rights. Self-ownership and the state are reconciled. Thus Locke bases the obligation to obey the state on our consent to the sovereign: on a social contract.

From this argument we can see Locke's account of the point of the state, and also the proper extent of its powers. The state is created in order to protect natural rights given by the law of nature, and so the state itself has no authority to interfere with these rights. Any attempt by the state to do so goes beyond its legitimate authority. It is obvious why Locke's conclusions are so congenial to Nozick.

How plausible is Locke's claim that legitimate authority can be based on the consent of the people? If we are to base legitimate authority on the consent of all the governed, then it is crucial to show that people actually do consent to their governments. But clearly there is, in general, no written or verbal contract made between individuals and their governments. Of course people may, on various occasions, swear their allegiance, but it is scarcely conceivable that any state has ever received universal express consent. Thus Locke requires a different concept of consent, and this need motivates his doctrine that although not everyone expressly consents to the state, nevertheless we do *tacitly* consent to it, by accepting benefits. By way of illustration, Locke argues:

> Every Man that hath any Possession, or Enjoyment, of any part of the Dominions of any Government, doth thereby give his tacit Consent, and is as far forth obliged to Obedience to the Laws of that Government, during such enjoyment, as any one under it; whether this his Possession be of Land to him and his Heirs for ever, or a Lodging only for a Week; or whether it be barely travelling freely on the Highway.[5]

The general idea that people are bound to the state only if they consent to it is one which the defender of self-ownership would surely find attractive. If any state could be defended on the grounds that all its citizens actually and expressly consent un-coerced, then it is hard to see how even the anarchist could object. But to be told, first, that tacit consent is considered a sufficient form of consent, and, second, that the mere acceptance of apparently unavoidable benefits constitutes tacit consent, will drain the doctrine of appeal. But why? What is so unsatisfactory about the idea of tacit consent as a form of consent? One obvious thought is that if people are said to consent, then one necessary condition seems to be that dissent must be a realistic option. In the case of tacit consent, to dissent would be to refuse the benefits offered, in effect to leave the country, and the protection of the state. But, as Hume pointed out:

> Can we seriously say, that a poor peasant or artizan has a free choice to leave his country, when he knows no foreign language or manners, and lives from day to day, by the small wages which he acquires? We may as well assert, that a man, by remaining in a vessel, freely consents to the dominion of the master; though he was carried on board while asleep, and must leap into the ocean, and perish, the moment he leaves her.[6]

In sum, then, Hume and others argue that even if we do accept benefits from the state, this cannot properly be construed as tacitly consenting to it. Thus Locke's doctrine of tacit consent will not convince the self-ownership theorist that the state is morally legitimate. If Nozick is to find a way to justify the state and refute the anarchist, that way cannot be Locke's.

Nozick's Invisible Hand

Nozick's approach to the Lockean predicament is to present the case that, if one looks at it hard enough, one will find that it does not exist. While he agrees that Locke has pointed to important problems with the state of nature, Nozick argues that Locke's dismissal of anarchy is too quick. First of all, we should see whether the state of nature has its own remedies for dealing with its difficulties. Are there any methods for the efficient administration of justice within the state of nature? Nozick's central contention, and one of his original contributions to this debate, is that the state of nature does allow such methods but when they are all employed we will, in effect, find ourselves with a state. This is the essence of his 'invisible hand explanation' of the state.

The basic idea of an invisible-hand explanation is to show how something that looks designed may nevertheless arise or evolve as an unintended consequence of other action. So Nozick argues that individuals in the state of nature, in trying to improve their position, will perform actions which will eventually bring about a minimal state, although no one intended this, or perhaps even thought about the creation of a state. To emphasize the point, Nozick subtitles Part 1 of *Anarchy, State, and Utopia* 'How to back into a state without really trying'. Later in this chapter I will argue that Nozick's use of the invisible hand methodology is ultimately dispensible to his argument, obscuring its real force. Nevertheless, it is necessary to pursue the argument through its intricate steps, in order to uncover the genuine insights it contains. Further, by following Nozick's line of thought here, we can admire him at his most ingenious.

Nozick, then, argues that the minimal state would emerge from the anarchic state of nature (if people were rationally self-interested and prepared, for the most part, to abide by the moral law), and, he adds, it could so emerge without violating anyone's rights. Two questions arise immediately. Are these claims true, and, if they are, what do they show? Suppose that if we were in the state of nature we would eventually bring about a minimal state without violating anyone's rights. Would this be enough to show that the minimal state is justified even if it actually arose in some other way? This is what Nozick seems to claim, and this methodological question will be discussed in detail shortly. Let us first see why Nozick thinks that the minimal state would arise from the state of nature and could do so without violating rights. There is, of course, no problem imagining how it might emerge in a rights-violating way – by conquest or force, for example – but it is the possibility of an immaculate conception, as it has been called,[7] which Nozick wishes to establish.

Later we will attempt a detailed critical assessment of Nozick's argument, but first we should try to understand the structure of that argument so we can see exactly what it is we are being offered. Like Nozick I shall present the argument in terms of a quasi-historical process by which the state develops, following the argument through a series of stages, beginning with the state of nature and ending with the minimal state. The argument rests, in part, on the claim that transition from each stage to the next occurs in such a way that no one's rights are violated.

From the State of Nature to the Dominant Agency

We must start with a reminder of the nature of the problems presented by the state of nature. Expanding on Locke's point that in the state of nature everyone is their own judge, Nozick reasons:

> Men who judge in their own case will always give themselves the benefit of the doubt and assume that they are in the right. They will overestimate the amount of harm or damage they have suffered, and passions will lead them to attempt to punish others more than proportionately and to exact excessive compensation ... [leading] to an endless series of acts of retaliation and exactions of compensation. And there is no firm way to *settle* such a dispute.... Even if one party *says* he'll stop his acts of retaliation, the other can rest secure only if he knows that the first does not feel entitled to gain recompense or to exact retribution.... Such feelings of being mutually wronged can occur even with the clearest right and with joint agreement on the facts of each person's conduct; all the more is

Hatfield
-McCoy
dilemma

there opportunity for such retaliatory battle when the facts or rights
are to some extent unclear. Also, in a state of nature a person may
lack the power to enforce his rights; he may be unable to punish or
exact compensation from a stronger adversary who has violated
them. (11–12)

How, then, may people in the state of nature attempt to resolve
these difficult problems? The most natural idea is that an individual
may band with others in a 'mutual protection association'. 'Others
may join with him in his defence, at his call. They may join ...
because they are public spirited, or because they are his friends, or
because he has helped them in the past, or because they wish him
to help them in the future, or in exchange for something' (12). This
way, at least, justice might be exacted from a stronger violator, or
protection gained against unreasonable claims. Our first quasi-
historical progression, then, is from the state of nature to a
situation in which there exists mutual protection associations.

(1)

Do mutual protection associations present any advantages over
the state of nature? Don't they just reproduce the problems at the
level of gang, rather than individual, warfare? Remember, however, we never were supposing a condition of thoroughgoing
individual warfare, only a situation where people have trouble
agreeing whether rights violations have taken place, and what the
fitting punishment and compensation should be. The mutual
protection association may well have at least one advantage over
this initial situation: co-members may be unwilling to co-operate
with a claimant unless they feel that the case is a reasonable one.
Not being blinded by self-love or passion, they will not wish to
waste time and effort pursuing a claim that has little merit.
Consequently, one would expect fewer unreasonable disputes.

This advantage is tempered by a disadvantage: pursuing any
claim on behalf of a fellow member involves the expenditure of
time and effort, and this is something most would prefer to avoid.
The answer, says Nozick, is the division of labour. In true
free-marketeering fashion, he proposes that entrepreneurs could
set up in business to provide protection services. Rather than
securing protection by joining in a mutual protection association
with others, one could purchase the services of a protection
agency. This is the third stage: the setting up of commercial
protection agencies.[8] Presumably many would choose to hire the
expert services of others, rather than form an association in which

(2)

one is constantly at the call of other members.

Initially, in any geographic area, competing agencies would offer their services. But Nozick argues that this is one free market which has a tendency to monopoly, or at least, oligopoly. We will examine the argument for this later on, but the basic idea is that competing agencies would find it in their interests to merge, or make agreements to co-operate, so that disputes between members of different agencies can be settled by arbitration, rather than by mutually costly battle. There is also an advantage for the consumer in joining the biggest, most powerful, agency. Thus, by a process of mergers, take-overs, cartels, and changing membership patterns we will arrive, in effect, at a fourth stage, at a situation in which there is one dominant protection agency, or a federation of co-operating agencies, in any geographical location.

Having now arrived at the existence of a dominant protection agency, have we, at this point, backed into a state without really trying? That is, is the dominant protection agency a state? We saw in Chapter 2 that one feature of the state is that it claims a monopoly of force. Does a dominant protection agency claim this? It is plausible that a protection agency may require that members renounce the right to exact punishment personally, or, in some circumstances, to defend themselves, as a condition of membership, so that the conduct of disputes remains always under the control of the agency. But, it appears, not everyone need be a member of the protection agency. Some strongly individualistic people – John Wayne types – may refuse to buy such a service, being prepared to defend themselves and punish others should the need arise. Of course, we could question how successful they are likely to be, but the point remains that it is hard to see how, in a libertarian view, someone could be compelled to give up the natural right to punish. And if at least some individuals retain the private right to punish, the dominant protection agency apparently is not a state. In addition the dominant protection agency does not possess the second feature demanded of a state: the provision of protection services to all. John Wayne, if he does not buy protection services, must look after himself. Is the dominant protection agency, then, as far as Nozickian rights in a state of nature can take us in the direction of the state?

The Ultra-Minimal State and the Minimal State

Nozick has not yet run out of ideas. How might the protective agency and its clients deal with John Wayne, he asks. We need to ask another question before we can understand this one. What problem, if any, does John Wayne present? In other words, what is there to deal with? The answer, presumably, is that he presents exactly those problems found with the original state of nature. In exercising his rights to self-defence and punishment he may be blinded by self-love, or the revenge motive, and so exceed the decrees of the law of nature, punishing the wrong people, or over-punishing the right ones.

Is this a problem for the dominant agency? Why not simply wait and see if he does go beyond the law of nature in seeking private justice against its clients, and if he does, then punish him and make him pay compensation. But must the agency wait? If there is a risk that members' rights will be violated, may the agency act first, to make sure this does not happen? May the agency, in other words, prohibit private rights enforcement against its clients unless it can be assured that this enforcement does not itself violate rights? It is extremely risky to us all if there are people like John Wayne around particularly if one cannot be sure that they will always be motivated by calm reason. To protect its clients against such risks the dominant agency seems entitled to announce that it will punish anyone who uses force against its clients, unless they can demonstrate to the agency that such force is legitimate.

Notice what has happened at this point. There now exists an agency which claims a monopoly to authorize force. It will be the sole user of force on behalf of its clients, and sole authorizer of force used by independents against its clients.[9] We have now transcended the dominant protection agency and reached a fifth stage in which the dominant organization possesses one of the two features said to be central to the existence of the state: monopoly of authorized violence. For this reason Nozick argues that we should say that we have now arrived at the ultra-minimal state.

But matters cannot rest here. John Wayne has a natural right to punish others, but the dominant agency refuses to allow him to exercise this right because of the risk of harm he will do misusing that right. But, Nozick argues, if it prohibits him from using his natural right the dominant agency must compensate him for this.

The most appropriate form of compensation, in the circumstances, is to provide him with protection services. When the ultra-minimal state offers protection to those whom it prohibits from using force it becomes a state: the minimal state. Offering protection to all who reside within its boundaries is Nozick's second central feature of statehood.

Notice, too, that in providing services to all, the state appears to be engaging in redistributive activity – making some pay for services provided to others – yet the reason behind this is not redistributive. That is, the minimal state does not compel some to pay for the protection of others on the basis that otherwise those people would be unprotected. Rather, they must pay compensation for not allowing those others to exercise their natural rights, and the most convenient form of compensation is to provide protection services for them. So the reason for redistribution is not based on considerations of welfare, or equality, but on considerations of natural rights recognized by the libertarian.

We have, by a series of gradual stages, reached the minimal state, which claims a monopoly on force while protecting all. This is Nozick's invisible-hand argument for the state. No one in the state of nature intended to bring about the state, but it comes into existence anyway. At no stage in the transition, it is claimed, are any rights violated, and so, apparently, we have backed into a state without really trying. Nozick's argument has been called 'the most important attempt in this century to rebut anarchism and to justify the State'.[10] But before we can assess whether the attempt succeeds, we must first look more closely at how the argument is supposed to work.

Nozickian Methodology

What does Nozick's argument purport to show? In one sense, if Nozick is right, then the anarchist is refuted, for the argument demonstrates that there could be a morally legitimate state. It would be legitimate if it developed from the state of nature via Nozick's invisible-hand process. But if this is all Nozick wishes to show one might wonder why he went to the trouble of inventing a new argument. As we have seen, Locke and the social contract theorists have already shown the anarchist how a morally legitimate state *could* come about without violating libertarian rights:

we all make a contract to bring the state into existence.

So Nozick is obviously trying to establish something stronger than Locke's bare possibility claim.[11] But what? One idea is that he is arguing not merely for the possibility of a legitimate minimal state, but, as it were, for its moral necessity. That is, the minimal state is the *only* legitimate form of social organization. Now although Nozick certainly believes something like this, it is important to appreciate that he does not expect to establish the unique legitimacy of the minimal state solely on the basis of his invisible-hand argument. Rather, the argument for that conclusion has two stages. First, it is argued that *at least* the minimal state is justified, and then that *at most* the minimal state is justified. Together these separate arguments, of course, deliver the conclusion that only the minimal state is justified. The second stage is carried out by Nozick's argument that any more extensive state will violate people's rights to property, and we shall look at this in the next chapter. The invisible-hand argument, then, is designed to perform only the first task of showing to the anarchist that the minimal state, possibly among other forms of state, is justified. The 'uniqueness' result will have to wait.

How, then, is the argument against the anarchist supposed to work? It may appear rather simple. One just shows that the state is better than anarchy. More fully, first one describes the most 'favoured' form of non-state situation, which Nozick takes to be Locke's state of nature. This, rather than, say idyllic harmony, is chosen, because this is 'the best that realistically can be hoped for' (5). Things might be much worse without the state than Locke envisaged, but few can honestly believe that they would be much better. Having an account of the best realistic anarchy, Nozick suggests that

> If one could show that the state would be superior even to [the] most favoured situation of anarchy, the best that realistically can be hoped for, or would arise by a process involving no morally impermissible steps, or would be an improvement if it arose, this would provide a rationale for the state's existence; it would justify the state. (5)

We should note, however, that Nozick's actual methodology is, or at least should be, more strict than revealed by this comment, which seems to suggest several alternative possible justifications for the state. As we have already seen, showing that the state is superior to anarchy will not be enough, on Nozick's view, to justify the state, for it also must be shown to violate no rights. This, of course, is the force of the Lockean predicament. But in effect Nozick's contention is that if we could show that the state would emerge by a process involving no morally impermissible steps, *and* would be an improvement if it arose, this would justify the state. Both claims are necessary, for as Nozick also points out, if the state was seen as a deterioration from the state of nature, rather than an improvement, the fact that it would emerge without violating rights would hardly seem to justify it.

Although this may seem an attractive approach to the issue of the defence of the state there is one important stumbling-block. Why should we be interested in what would – hypothetically – develop from a hypothetical situation of anarchy? The anarchist would argue that the point is not what would or would not happen in some hypothetical state of affairs, but what has actually happened. Most existing states have their origin in force, conquest, revolution, or civil war. The anarchist may well conclude that such a foundation on violence is enough to make any state so founded immoral, irrespective of what would develop from the state of nature.[12]

How can Nozick demonstrate to the anarchist that these worries about the actual genesis of the state are beside the point? Nozick himself says very little to make this clear, and much of what he does say serves more to confuse than to illuminate. In particular, in the early pages of *Anarchy, State, and Utopia* Nozick draws a parallel between the structure of his argument and an idea of Hempel's, which Nozick terms a 'potential explanation'. Hempel's much discussed theory of explanation is, briefly, that to explain why something happened is to deduce it from a statement of laws and initial conditions. So, for example:

> To an observer in a rowboat, that part of an oar which is under water appears to be bent upwards. The phenomenon is explained by means of general laws – mainly the law of refraction and the law that water is an optically denser medium than air – and by reference to certain antecedent conditions – especially the facts that part of the oar is in the water, part in the air, and that the oar is practically a straight piece of wood. Thus ... the question '*Why* does the phenomenon occur?' is construed as meaning 'according to what general laws, and by virtue of what antecedent conditions does the phenomenon occur?'[13]

Nozick defines a *potential* explanation as 'what would be the correct explanation if everything in it were true and operated' (7). Thus, a potential explanation is a valid deduction of what is to be explained from perhaps false laws, non-existent facts, or processes which did not happen. It appears to some commentators[14] that Nozick suggests he has justified the state by providing a potential explanation for it and, indeed, the invisible-hand explanation can plausibly be said to be a potential explanation of the state. However this suggestion offers little help with the task of refuting the anarchist. A careful examination of Nozick's text reveals that he does not try to *defend* the state this way,[15] and a little reflection makes clear that such an attempt, on its own, would obviously fail. To explain why something happened is not, in itself, to justify it – to explain why it *ought to* have happened, or why it happened legitimately. A historian explaining why American slavery existed is not necessarily trying to justify it; indeed the opposite may be the case. But if a genuine explanation is not sufficient for moral justification, what hope is there for a potential explanation?

To make any real progress here we must step back and do what Nozick omits to do: place the discussion in the context of the problem of political obligation considered more generally.[16] We can raise the problem, first of all, with the questions: 'Why should I obey the dictates of the government? What authority does it have over me?' The anarchist intuition that the state has no such authority, we have seen, underlies Nozick's whole project, and is one side of what I have called the Lockean predicament. However, the other side of that predicament has also made its presence felt in this chapter. As Locke argues, if there is a state things are likely to go better, particularly in the area of the administration of justice. Thus I have good reason to welcome the existence of the state, and, in principle, to accept its authority over me, provided most others do too. We might say that when I appreciate these reasons I hypothetically consent to the state. If I were asked, my considered judgement would be that I do consent to many of its activities. This is why, for most of us, the original anarchist intuition has more philosophical interest than practical.

However, even if I am convinced that the government can legitimately interfere in certain of my affairs, other people may not be convinced that it has the right to interfere in theirs. It may be that they simply cannot be argued away from the anarchist intuition. If so, they will refuse to accept the state's authority. But of course no actually existing state would be prepared to accept that its jurisdiction is limited only to those who are prepared to accept that authority. Thus it is likely the state will force such dissenters to submit, and it is also likely that in this behaviour its action would have the approval of those who do support the state. But can the state legitimately use force in this way, or do we simply and immorally have a case of 'might' pretending to be 'right'? Thus the question of political obligation appears again, in a new and urgent form: what right does the state have to enforce the law against would-be independents?

If this approach to the problem of political obligation is accepted, then it is reasonable to see the task of justifying the state as falling into two stages. The first is to show that rational people have good reason to consider themselves bound to the state. To carry out this task will primarily be to demonstrate the advantages the state has over the state of nature: 'that it would be an improvement if it arose', so it would be rational for people to give it their consent. The second, and more difficult task is to show that even those who fail to be convinced by the argument for the state are, nevertheless, still morally bound to obey it, and therefore forcing their obedience violates no rights. One function of Locke's doomed doctrine of tacit consent is to fulfil this task by suggesting that even those who say they object *really* consent.

With this discussion in mind, and in particular the distinction between the two stages in the defence of the state, we can take stock of Nozick's argument and appreciate its real innovation and force. Nozick's invisible-hand process naturally falls into two parts. The first takes us from the state of nature to the dominant protection agency, and the second from the dominant protection agency to the minimal state. We can construe these two stages as representing answers to our two questions of political obligation. Nozick's answer to the question of why I should accept the authority of the state is that, in effect, if I consider the alternatives – private enforcement or mutual aid associations – I will realize, most likely, that the existence of the state to administer justice and enforce rights is far and away the most effective system, even though I must pay my share of it. In other words, the development from the state of nature to the dominant agency is the way in which the rational superiority of the state is demonstrated.

If Nozick is correct about the rational superiority of the state, then there will be those for whom the state needs no further justification, and who will be prepared to accept its authority: to consent to the state. But there will also be those like John Wayne, who nevertheless prefer the independent life. Perhaps if you are tough, or value self-reliance above all, or are very good at keeping out of trouble, then you may feel that the state has nothing to offer, and so you have no reason to consent to its existence. Indeed you may even believe that the existence of a powerful state is more dangerous to you than anarchy. So if John Wayne would not consent to the state, what right do we have to compel his submission? Here, as we have seen, Nozick's answer is that we are entitled to prohibit John Wayne from engaging in the risky activity of privately enforcing his rights, but we must compensate him for this by offering him protection services. Thus prohibition and compensation move us from the situation where only those who would consent are bound and protected, to the situation where *all* are bound to obey the state and are protected by it, at least where matters of the administration of justice are concerned.

If my interpretation is correct, then we should recognize that although Nozick's answer to the problem of political obligation is stated in terms of a hypothetical process, this has as much to do with Nozick's desire for elegance and novelty in presentation, and with his fascination with the idea of invisible-hand processes, as with the actual content of his theory. Nozick could have presented his solution – less stylishly – without mentioning invisible hands, potential explanations, or hypothetical processes. Although in some places these devices do aid the exposition, they also obscure it, and if Nozick had proceeded more plainly, perhaps his innovative ideas would generally be better understood. What I propose to do is to reconstruct the argument in a way that lays bare its crucial steps.

In summary, Nozick owes answers to two questions. First, is it rational for people to accept the authority of the state? Second, can those who nevertheless prefer independence also rightfully be compelled to submit? Concentrating on the first of these questions, I take Nozick's position to be that it is rational, and this is shown by the fact that the vast majority of people placed in Locke's state of nature would voluntarily contract into the situation where an entity very similar to the state exists. Our immediate tasks are to examine if this is so, and also, if this establishes the rational acceptability of the state. We can then turn to the second question.

The Rational Acceptability of the State

We begin in the state of nature with the problem of how to administer justice, bearing in mind that each person is his or her own judge. The first transition is to a situation in which individuals band together for mutual protection, seeking to aid each other in their struggles for justice.

It is, at this point, worth raising a general worry articulated by various critics of Nozick. How do we know what transitions are plausible until we know what people are like? There are two points here. First, without some description of the psychology of the beings under consideration we may have no idea of what they will do, and second, there may be no universal truth to be had here. A territory full of misanthropes would surely evolve in a quite different fashion to one of more sociable creatures.

However, it is important to make clear that Nozick is not offering us a theory of historical development. He does not set out to predict how actual human beings will behave; he is concerned only with those who are rationally self-interested but generally prepared to respect the rights of others. This is why Nozick does not spend time on psychological and sociological questions, and why, implicitly, he is content with the abstract rational being of game theory and economics, whose psychology is primarily constituted by the assumptions of those disciplines.[17] If these assumptions are not sufficiently accurate 'idealizations' of human rationality then Nozick's argument will not tell us what rational people in the state of nature would choose to do. But here, rational choice theory in general (including large parts of economic theory and the other social sciences) is equally vulnerable, and it is wrong to single Nozick out as being especially so, once the nature of his project is recognized.

There seems little to object to in the first transition from the state of nature to mutual protection associations, once we accept that people have the natural rights Nozick supposes. Certainly banding together with others to help administer justice seems rational enough. We need note only two assumptions required to support this step: first, that individuals can transfer to other people their rights to defend themselves and to punish transgressors; second, that all have the right to enforce the natural law, even if it is the rights of others which are under threat. Strictly, of course, once the second assumption is made, the first is unnecessary. The second assumption is required to allow 'the public spirited' to join in to help the unjustly treated, as Nozick suggests they might. Although this assumption was granted by Locke, the individualist anarchist may well worry, as Nozick recognizes, that it could lead to intrusive intervention into private concerns. Nevertheless, even without assuming a general right to punish, little in practice is lost, provided the assumption that rights may be transferred is accepted. The public spirited may join the lynching mob once they are invited.[18]

The transition from these mutual protection associations to commercial protection agencies is a little more challenging. To many it appears to rely on a degree of sophistication unlikely to be enjoyed by those in the state of nature. However, there is no reason in principle why this development should not take place. If there is to be private property in the state of nature, then there may be exchange, money, and the sale of various services. Protection services may, in that case, be a relatively early invention. The only obvious requirement is that we agree to private property rights. However, without private property rights the administration of justice may create less difficulty and so the need for the state would be diminished. Further, such rights are generally assumed within the natural rights tradition. Whether the assumption is justified is, of course, a different question, to be discussed in Chapter 4.

There does, however, appear to be one serious problem with this transition. Protection services are going to be expensive.[19] A protection agency requires full-time expert personnel to carry out and administer the detection of crime and its fair assessment, just as actually existing states require vast human resources to carry out these tasks. Now, if the state of nature is populated by the poor, then people may simply be unable to afford such protection services, even if they want them. So there are circumstances in which the transition to commercial agencies will not be made.

What this objection shows is that Nozick assumes there is a reasonable amount of wealth in the state of nature.[20] This is a further reason for believing that Nozick is not talking about any actual historical development. Instead, if we see Nozick as answering the anarchist's question 'why should I accept the authority of the state?' then the only people whose wealth should be taken into account are the person asking the question and those other members of that person's society. So Nozick's answer to most people reading the book is likely to be: you would prefer the state and you, and most people around you, can afford it. This is shown by the fact that you all, or almost all, would contract into a protection agency if you were in the state of nature. If this understanding of the argument is seen as persuasive, the assumption that people in the state of nature are not so poor as to be unable to purchase protection seems justified.

But should we not know how these protection agencies would behave before we decide whether to buy their services? What would a protection agency have to be like in order to flourish? One thought is that the most popular sort of protection agencies will be those that offer a 'no questions asked' service, prepared to pursue claims irrespective of considerations of justice. This idea prompts Bernard Williams's complaint that in all likelihood protection agencies would be 'partial towards their clients, hypocritical towards potential clients, and horrible towards confirmed non-clients'.[21] But we must, as Williams also notes, remember that we are considering Nozick's 'best realistic' form of anarchy, in which rights violations are the exception, not the rule. So although some may choose to become clients of an outlaw agency, others would view its existence with repugnance, boycotting it, and otherwise refusing to co-operate. Other agencies may gang up to truncate its activities. There is, then, little reason to believe that such agencies would flourish, given Nozick's assumptions.

We may assume that there would exist few agencies prepared to violate rights on behalf of a client. But why should there not be a specialist agency for rich clients, prepared, like some lawyers, to push matters as far as they can go without violating rights, and who will rarely, if ever, concede defeat? Could these 'unreasonable', though not, strictly speaking, immoral, agencies survive?

The answer to this, perhaps, depends on the accuracy of Nozick's observation that the market for protection services carries with it a natural tendency to monopoly. Thus, is Nozick right to posit a third progression from competing commercial agencies to a single dominant agency? If he is, then specialist 'unreasonable' agencies, and all agencies except the one which becomes dominant, will be crushed by market forces. Nevertheless, it might still be open to a dominant agency to sell protection policies of differing strengths.

The Problem of Monopoly

In a way it is surprising for a libertarian to argue that any market has a natural tendency to monopoly. One recurring theme of anarchist and liberal *laissez-faire* thought is that monopolies can only be maintained by state power: by licensing systems, for example. In the state of nature the free market would be expected to lead to a situation of perfect competition, in which many different suppliers compete to supply each type of good.

Two factors, however, suggest that this would not be true of the market for protection services. As mentioned before, it would be in the interests of each agency to come to agreements with others about how they will resolve disputes. If they can agree a procedure, this will save costly battles. Therefore agencies have an incentive to form larger associations or to merge. Also, it must not be forgotten that consumers are buying *protection* services, and the effectiveness of such a service will depend, in part, on the resources that the agency can command. This, again in part, is a function of the size of the agency: how many people it is paid to protect. Other things being equal, people will seek out the largest agency as this will be best able to protect them. It seems that by this process eventually one agency will become dominant and command a monopoly.

One problem with this second argument is that it assumes a simple relation between the size of the agency and the ability it has to protect each member. This ignores the fact that by charging huge sums for protection, some agencies – perhaps 'unreasonable agencies' – may be able to command vast resources yet have very few clients. More importantly, there exists what we might call bureaucratic friction. Although a large agency may be *able* effectively to press claims on behalf of its clients, whether it *will* do so depends on how well organized it is. Perhaps small, streamlined agencies which offer a 'personal service' may be more effective, if more expensive. Of course such agencies may lose out in all-out war, but perhaps they will not – guerrilla bands and organized gangs survive against the power of the state – and war is unlikely if the law of nature is to be observed. I can see no obvious way of determining whether individuals would consider themselves better served by a single, large agency, or a small agency offering a less bureaucratic service.

For these reasons it seems to me that the first argument for monopoly, based on the advantages to be obtained from solving disputes by arbitration, is the safer. Thus an oligarchy or federation of agencies may develop, which, rather than doing battle, agree to some sort of courtroom procedure. Accordingly protection agencies may gain a monopoly in the way professional associations now possess them. Dentists are all members of a professional body, and in that sense form a monopoly. Nevertheless, one may choose which member of that profession one employs. We may speak of a dominant agency at least in this sense, and it is also possible that advantages of scale will provide a force by which a single agency genuinely becomes dominant. Let us, for the sake of the argument, assume that it will, while noting the reservation that this has not been proved.

We are, however, left with a very awkward question. If Nozick is right and there will emerge one dominant agency, what guarantee is there that it will not exploit its monopoly position and charge an unreasonable price for its services? The normal response is that other firms will rush in to undercut the monopolist, but if Nozick is right that here we have a *natural* monopoly, then small firms will simply be unable to compete.

This objection raises a general worry about Nozick's argument. We may be convinced by the argument that rational people in the state of nature will bring about the situation where a dominant protection agency exists. This may happen, say, when each person joins a small agency and then, after a process of mergers and takeovers, one agency becomes dominant. But it does not follow from this that it is rational to accept the dominant protection agency. Perhaps when the monopolist agency, charging whatever maximizes its profit, gains dominance, people will sorely regret that they ever gave up their independence. Even though choosing to join a protection agency seemed a very good idea, if we now bear in mind what the protection agency has turned into, the state of nature may, after all, be preferable. As Locke pointed out, in taking care 'to avoid what Mischiefs may be done them by Pole-Cats or Foxes', people must avoid being 'devoured by Lions'.[22]

We might draw an analogy with another problem of a similar structure. I might decide to purchase a car so I can travel to work more quickly than by taking the bus. But when everyone makes a similar decision, traffic congestion becomes unbearable, and the bus company goes out of business. So we all end up getting to work more slowly than before, although considered in isolation each decision seems wholly rational.[23] Thus, returning to the issue of the dominant protection agency, whatever we want to say about the rationality of the initial decision to join, the essential point remains that even though people arrived at the dominant agency through, in a sense, their own free choices, they may, nevertheless, later have good reason to regret those choices.

Nozick has little to say in answer to these problems. However here, possibly, he misses a trick. The way to head off this type of objection is to make the dominant agency rationally desirable in itself, rather than merely the inevitable outcome of a set of apparently rational choices. One way to do this is to reconceive the relation between the agency and its clients. There are at least two possible roles for these clients to play. One is the role of 'customer', purchasing protection from the agency. Here, then, the only control the client has over the agency is that given by the market, and if the agency is a monopoly, then that control is practically nil. However, we can also think of individuals as members, rather like shareholders, in the organization. If so, they can bring the organization to account for its activities, force it to change its pricing policy, or vote new 'directors' on to the board. This way members can exert rigorous control over the agency in a way in which the market is unable to do, and so, in principle, they may remove any undesirable feature the agency may develop. In addition to being more rationally desirable than Nozick's conception of the dominant agency, this has what many would see as the advantage of making room for something much more like the modern democratic state. Indeed, it is sometimes noted that, as it stands, Nozick's political philosophy seems to leave no place for politics, for there are apparently no political procedures at all within the minimal state.[24] However recasting the relation between the agency and its members in the way I have suggested goes some way to make good this omission. Electing officers at the Annual General Meeting is a good representation of a Parliamentary Election.

Interesting though these matters are, there is, nevertheless, a question of how much of the detail of this argument is necessary to establish the conclusion that the state is rationally defensible. Perhaps we should see the argument simply as a way of making very plain the second half of the Lockean predicament. Thus we can imagine Nozick saying to the anarchist: although you are correct that natural rights appear to lead to anarchy, just look at the advantages of the existence of the state, at least in certain forms. It is generally rational to prefer the state to anarchy, and thus to give your consent to the state. The anarchist may reply: Whether or not it is rational, I prefer anarchy. And as I am not prepared to consent, expressly, tacitly, or hypothetically, to the state, then if it compels me to obey, it violates my natural rights. It is his reply to this challenge that distinguishes Nozick from the social contract theorists.

Compelling the Anarchist

At this point, then, the hard work begins. What do we say to those still unconvinced? This question is represented by the point that at this stage in the Nozickian process not all individuals need be members of the dominant agency: we called one such independent John Wayne. Nozick argues, we saw, that the dominant agency has a right to ban John Wayne from privately enforcing his rights. This is because he presents the risk that in over-enthusiastically pursuing his claims, he may either damage innocent parties, or punish the guilty beyond the licence of the law of nature.

Certainly John Wayne is dangerous. But is the agency justified in prohibiting him from exercising his natural rights? Does it violate his rights if it does this, or does he violate the rights of others by exposing them to risk? Perhaps, despite Nozick's efforts in setting up the structure of his rights theory, we are faced with the possibility of a clash of rights. One obvious attempt to sidestep this difficult question is the thought that a libertarian ought to feel comfortable banning John Wayne's dangerous private enforcement of justice on the grounds that we are justified in prohibiting any activity that might lead to a violation of rights. However, Nozick cannot make this response, for he argues that sometimes we should even allow activities which we know for certain will violate rights, provided compensation is paid.

The policy of sometimes allowing violations appears to sit uneasily with a libertarian account of the value of rights against aggression. In essence, as we saw, one has rights, according to libertarian theory, so that one may exercise rational autonomy and control one's own fate. Rights would be valueless for this purpose if they could be arbitrarily violated, provided only that compensation is paid. Nozick also briefly makes this point, albeit in a way which rather curiously appears to blend libertarian and utilitarian reasoning: 'A system permitting boundary crossing, provided compensation is paid, embodies the use of persons as means; knowing they are being so used, and that their plans and expectations are liable to be thwarted arbitrarily, is a cost to people' (71).

Nevertheless, Nozick points to circumstances in which rights can be violated without plans being thwarted: without treating people as means. It would take us too far afield to follow Nozick's thought in detail here, but it is not hard to think of cases where the policy of 'violate first, compensate later' may seem entirely appropriate. One type of case suggests itself to Nozick: where for some sort of technical reason it is not possible to get the consent of the rights holder, although there is good reason to suppose that the rights holder would consent to an exchange if it were offered. Or it may be possible to get permission, but extremely costly, perhaps so costly that it will eat up the profits generated by the transaction. Another important case is that in which one party does not even know whose consent it is they must obtain. Here the costs of finding out may again be prohibitively high.

Summarizing Nozick's arguments, only a few of which I have mentioned, we can tentatively draw an incomplete, though complex, conclusion on Nozick's behalf. If an action involving a rights violation would produce great benefit, and it is extremely costly or impossible to obtain in advance the consent of the rights holder, and there is no reason to suppose that the rights holder would refuse to consent (on appropriate terms) if approached, and the benefits of the exchange will be fairly divided, and a system allowing such violations would not create great fear,[25] then rights violations should be permitted, provided compensation is paid. This complex principle is, of course, incomplete, as we have no precise criteria for 'great benefit',[26] 'extreme cost', 'fair division', and 'great fear'. And the principle is only tentatively attributed to Nozick for he does not say whether such a principle would treat people as means, nor does he give us any information about how we should decide the issue. Perhaps he believes that provided there is no reason to think that consent would be refused on suitable terms, the principle does not treat people as means.

Nozick does not, then, believe that we should punish all rights violations. He cannot, therefore, argue that we should prohibit all

activity which carries with it the risk of violating rights. Nevertheless, he argues that we are entitled to prohibit John Wayne's risky
activity. On what basis can he do this?

Risk and Procedural Rights

We do not apply the same policy to every case of risk. Consider
first Nozick's case of someone who wishes to play Russian roulette
on unwilling strangers. Even if such a person offers to compensate
all victims we would, nevertheless, surely be entitled simply to
prohibit this strange and risky practice. But it would be absurd to
extend this policy to all actions which carry some risk of rights
violation. In driving my car I am taking the risk of violating the
rights of others, such as pedestrians, and even by walking on a
country path I risk violating other people's private property rights
by accidentally straying on to their land. All activity, it appears,
carries with it some risk, however small, of violating another's
rights.

Sometimes we do prohibit risky activity. In other cases we allow
risky activity provided compensation is paid for any harm caused.
In the case of car driving, we take a third approach: we allow the
action to take place, provided that procedures are followed which
minimize risk and that the driver can demonstrate that adequate
funds are available to compensate anyone injured. This is the point
of making car insurance compulsory. But as we have seen, the
corner-stone of Nozick's argument for the minimal state is that a
fourth approach is the correct one to take to John Wayne: that the
dominant agency may prohibit him from engaging in the risky
business of private enforcement of justice, but must compensate
him for refusing to allow him to exercise his natural rights. The
first step – prohibition – takes us to the ultra-minimal state with its
monopoly of force, and the second – compensation – to the
minimal state in which all are protected.

It is, however, one thing to say that this is how to respond to
John Wayne, but quite another to demonstrate it from a natural
rights perspective. How do we know that we should not treat John
Wayne like the player of Russian roulette, or the driver of a car, or
the country walker? First of all, why should we prohibit John
Wayne from engaging in his risky activity?

Nozick attempts two distinct lines of argument to show that the

dominant agency may follow this policy. One argument introduces a new concept, specific to issues involving the administration
of justice: that of a procedural right. The other argument relies
only on more general considerations. Let us examine first the
argument based on procedural rights.

The basic idea of a procedural right is that, in general, one has a
right to a trial known to be fair. No one should act on the mere
assumption that another is guilty and deserving of punishment.
This is something which must be established or proved, and, in
law, we insist that this proof is demonstrated within a procedure
publicly known and available for inspection: the courts. Nozick
admits that 'The notions of procedural rights, public demonstration of guilt, and the like have a very unclear status within state of
nature theory' (96). Nevertheless, he adds, 'persons within this
tradition do not hold that there are *no* procedural rights; that is,
one may not defend oneself against being handled by unreliable or
unfair procedures' (101).

Assuming that people have procedural rights does not entail,
Nozick notes, that an accused person must actually approve of the
procedure being used to adjudicate his or her guilt. If this were the
case, criminals could avoid justice by refusing to accept any
procedure at all. Rather, it allows one to resist procedures known
to be unreliable – trial by ordeal, for example – and, perhaps, those
procedures not known to be reliable. One has a duty to submit to
procedures known to be reasonable. Known to whom? Assuming
that the dominant agency is not going to act outside the law of
nature, and has the 'muscle' to back its judgement, what is known
by the dominant agency may be decisive, and legitimately so,
suggests Nozick. He envisages that the agency will publish a list of
known, reliable procedures, and proclaim that anyone using
against its clients a procedure not on this list will be punished.

In sum, if people have the right to have their guilt assessed by a
procedure known to be reliable, then the agency may retain the
right to approve all judicial methods used against its clients. In
other words, the agency may set itself up as the sole authorizer of
coercion: it has become the ultra-minimal state.

Is Nozick correct in assuming that people have procedural
rights? He notes one response: assuming procedural rights makes
too easy the argument that the state may prohibit private enforcement of justice. Nozick's own concern is the question of whether
those people who know themselves to be guilty have the right to

have their guilt determined by a fair procedure. He believes that they do, and that the assumption of procedural rights is justified, but he realizes that others may be less charitable to this assumption, and so he produces an alternative argument which does not appeal to the idea. Let us first, however, look at some other objections to Nozick's use of the notion of a procedural right.

One objection, raised by Jeffrey Paul[27] is that, 'Typically, a procedural right is a convention defined within and granted by a particular legal code', and thus is a conventional right, not a natural right. The idea of procedural rights existing before the minimal state comes into being seems absurd. A second objection is that if there are natural procedural rights, then they exist from the very beginning of the state of nature. Thus, from the start everyone has the right to have their guilt assessed by a procedure known to be reliable, and so a plaintiff only has the right to pursue his or her claim if the reliability of the procedures adopted is demonstrated. Thus the administration of justice in the state of nature may present far fewer intractable disputes than Nozick supposes, if he is right to assume procedural rights.

On Nozick's behalf, however, it could be argued that these objections underestimate the importance of the idea of a procedural right. It is not unreasonable to argue that one's procedural rights are as firmly based as one's right to liberty, whatever the status of that right may be. Indeed the former may plausibly be said to be based upon the latter, for subjecting someone to an unfair trial is often thought to be a violation of their liberty. Therefore, in reply to the objections to procedural rights, we can say that although one does have the right to be tried by a method publicly known to be reasonably reliable, what that method will be is bound to vary from place to place. Thus there is room for some arbitrariness and divergences between conventions within the framework of the natural right to procedural justice. Further, although there may be procedural rights within the state of nature, it may also be true that no procedure is publicly known to be reliable. One of the problems concerning the administration of justice within the state of nature may be that procedural rights, inevitably, will often be violated.

Thus Nozick's view that the natural rights tradition should accept the concept of a procedural right seems defensible, but, partly to stave off objections from those less sympathetic, Nozick also attempts an alternative argument to the conclusion that John

Wayne's risky activity may be prohibited. This argument, which I think is less effective, does not appeal to any special considerations to do with the administration of justice, but relies on the view that the agency may treat John Wayne in the way it would treat anyone imposing a risk on its members.

How may it treat those that impose such risks? Nozick suggests that it may employ what he calls 'an epistemic principle of border crossing'. In its final version this states 'If someone knows that doing act A would violate Q's rights unless condition C obtained, he may not do A if he has not ascertained that C obtains through being in the best feasible position for ascertaining this' (106–7). He adds that anyone may punish a violator of this prohibition. Textual consideration show that by 'ascertained' Nozick appears to mean 'judged'.[28] Given this, the principle entails for John Wayne that he may not punish anyone unless he has followed the best feasible means of determining their guilt, and this means following the most reliable available procedure. Thus it can be wrong to punish even the guilty, unless one has put oneself in the best feasible situation to assess their guilt. This argument, then, produces a consequence similar to that achieved by the assumption of procedural rights – procedures known to be reliable must be followed – but without making that assumption.

But is the 'epistemic principle of border crossing' acceptable? Remember that Nozick said that the dominant agency may treat John Wayne as it treats anyone engaged in risky activity. So how may the dominant agency treat risky people? Nozick does not want to say that it has a right to prohibit all risky activity, for this would entail, as we saw, the prohibition of almost all we do. Further, he would not want to argue that all activity that risks serious harm must be prohibited, since, first, from a natural rights perspective all harm is serious, and second, some activities which impose 'normal' risks of death on others – driving for example – Nozick seems prepared to allow. Other risky activities, such as Russian roulette on the unwilling, are to be prohibited. The problem is, the epistemic principle of border crossing intrudes too far across too many borders.

By driving my car I risk violating rights of others. Certainly I have a duty to take as much care as I reasonably can to make sure that I will not interfere with anyone's rights, but what would it be to use the best feasible means for ascertaining that I will not violate rights? I am far less likely to violate the rights of the innocent if I employ a servant to walk in front of me, as I drive, waving a red flag, and warning me if anyone comes near. Perhaps four servants, in radio contact, carrying closed circuit cameras, would do an even better job. In other words, what do we mean by feasible? Is the best feasible means the best physically possible? If so, the libertarian must advocate radical changes in the Highway Code.

My suspicion is that we cannot give a firm criterion for 'best feasible' that accords with the policies we find desirable. We must reject the epistemic principle of boundary crossing, and hope other considerations may perform the required function. But as we have seen, if Nozick is right to assume procedural rights, then we appear to have good reason to prevent John Wayne's private enforcement of justice, unless he is supervised by the protection agency.

However, one point on this topic remains worth making. We noted before that we have different attitudes to different cases of risk, and nothing Nozick says indicates that he wishes to reform these attitudes. Indeed he uses some of our normal intuitions as arguments for his principles. The difficulty is how we can account for all these attitudes to risk within a libertarian framework. For example, one plausible explanation of why we permit people to drive cars, and thereby expose others to risk, is the great benefits to be derived from this activity. This is a utilitarian-style argument which cannot be adopted by Nozick without seriously compromising his moral theory. Indeed, within a theory so opposed to utilitarian reasoning it is hard to see how Nozick can distinguish between the risks of driving and of invasive Russian roulette. The lesson here is that libertarian theory may try to survive on too narrow a diet of values. We shall return to this issue shortly.

A Clash of Rights?

One essential matter remains in need of clarification. The crucial move in the argument, once we dismiss the epistemic principle of border crossing, is that those whom John Wayne wishes to punish have procedural rights, and he must respect these, even if it means that he cannot exercise his rights to punish as he wishes to. The question we have to ask is whether this is correctly represented as a clash of rights — a question Nozick never quite brings to the surface.

Given the discussion in Chapter 2, it may be asked how it could possibly be that within Nozick's structure of negative, side-constraint rights, a clash of rights could develop. The answer is that, as we saw, it is not clear whether we should view the right to punish as positive or negative. Essentially it is a right to interfere with others. Thus it should be no surprise that it might clash with rights to non-interference.

If we say that the issue of the conflict between procedural rights and self-defence is a clash of rights, this leads us to two problems, one specific to this argument, and one more general and more serious. The specific problem is that if John Wayne's rights to punish clash with the procedural rights of another, then what reason do we have for assuming that it is John Wayne's rights that must give way? An uncharitable thought is that Nozick appears to be assuming that, between clashing rights, force decides, as the protection agency has more power than any individual. But the anarchist is hardly likely to accept this as a justification of the state. More generally, if we have a clash of rights, then there is an incompleteness in libertarian political theory. Rights are not placed in a hierarchy of importance by Nozick, and politically, the only values to which we can appeal are rights. So it is not clear that there are any conceptual resources within Nozick's theory for adjudicating a clash of rights. If this is Nozick's final position, then the attractive simplicity of Nozick's political philosophy has an unattractive cost: insoluble political problems.

An alternative to admitting clashes of rights is to argue that the natural right to punish is always constrained or limited by procedural rights. If we take this view then to insist that John Wayne should respect the procedural rights of the accused does not violate his rights, for his rights are conditional in just this way. This suggestion seems pleasantly to tidy up the theory. However, as we shall see, this proposal too has its cost for Nozick's argument.

The Principle of Compensation

Even if Nozick is right that the ultra-minimal state would emerge without violating rights, he has still to show that it will develop into the minimal state. We saw, in outline, how the argument goes: the dominant agency may prohibit John Wayne from punishing others – this gives us the ultra-minimal state – but it must compensate him for this prohibition, and the best form of compensation is to offer him protective services. This gives us the minimal state in which the state protects all.

In making this final step Nozick uses what he calls the 'principle of compensation'. This states that 'those who are *disadvantaged* by being forbidden to do actions that only *might* harm others must be compensated for these disadvantages foisted upon them in order to provide security for the others' (82–3). We can see how this principle is to be applied to John Wayne: if he is disadvantaged by the prohibition of his risky activity, which only might harm others, then he must be compensated.

One thing we must note, as Nozick admits, is that this particular transition has a quite different character from those that went before it. All previous transitions have been the consequence of rational, self-interested behaviour. However, to get to the minimal state requires also a rather strong moral motivation: people must realize that they are morally obliged to compensate John Wayne for prohibiting his actions, and the recognition of this moral obligation must be sufficient for the members of the dominant agency to provide that compensation. No one else is going to force them to do so. Nozick gives us no reason to suppose that people will behave in this manner, and this surely would cast doubt on the plausibility of the transition, if it is intended historically. However, as I have insisted, we can best understand Nozick's invisible-hand process as a way of modelling questions and answers. The question here is whether the state has a duty to protect independents whom it has forbidden to protect themselves, and the answer given is that morally speaking, it ought to. Hence the objection that the state may not actually do this is beside the point.

More important, for our purposes, than the question of whether people will act in accordance with the principle of compensation is the question of whether that principle itself is acceptable and should be applied in this case. Nozick anticipates that it may cause some puzzlement. It might be objected that either you have a right to prohibit particular risky activities or you do not. If you do, you need not compensate, and, if you do not, you must not interfere. Thus, there is no place for a principle of compensation. In particular, if we understand the right to punish as being already constrained by procedural rights, as we considered in the last section, then prohibiting John Wayne from punishing unless he follows known procedures violates no rights. Thus, there is nothing for which he needs compensating. Hence to make compensation even relevant, Nozick needs to argue that John Wayne has rights which he is prevented from exercising as they conflict with the procedural rights of others. Let us, reserving our doubt, assume that Nozick is correct that in every such clash of rights procedural rights take priority. But can Nozick show that when John Wayne's right to punish is overruled, compensation must be paid?

Nozick is right to point out that there *may* be cases where we can legitimately prohibit risky action, provided that we pay some form of compensation. It is possible that the principle of compensation gives a plausible account of when this is so. If so, and if the principle applies in this case, then we have an argument for moving from the ultra-minimal to the minimal state. It is noteworthy, however, that Nozick does not give any arguments for the principle of compensation, nor is he able to derive it from other libertarian assumptions. So we need to examine whether the principle of compensation is, in general, acceptable, and one approach is to look at other cases to which it applies.

Nozick claims that sometimes an activity may be especially risky if a certain person does it, and so we may feel it appropriate to prohibit that person from performing that action, yet compensate for the disadvantage suffered. Nozick mentions the example of an epileptic who wants to drive a car. We feel entitled to prohibit this simply because of the extra risk involved, but '[P]rohibiting someone from driving in our automobile-dependent society, in order to reduce the risk to others, seriously disadvantages that person. It costs money to remedy these disadvantages – hiring a chauffeur or using taxis' (79). Thus, Nozick argues, we should compensate the epileptic for disadvantages suffered.

Intuitively we may well be sympathetic to this claim. We will not, as Nozick notes, be sympathetic to the claims of the would-be Russian roulette player who asks for compensation for the disadvantage of not getting the opportunity to play her favourite game on strangers. What explains our different judgements? For Nozick much rests on the concept of disadvantage – is the epileptic disadvantaged in a way in which the Russian roulette player is not? But what does Nozick mean by disadvantage? We must, in fact, distinguish between making someone worse off, and what Nozick calls disadvantaging them. Suppose that the epileptic driver is wealthy and prohibiting him from driving causes him no real hardship, because he can easily afford a chauffeur. In that case, while prohibiting him from driving costs him money, and so in one sense makes him worse off, we would not, according to Nozick, have disadvantaged him. Nozick admits that he does not make this concept of disadvantage very clear, but roughly the idea is that someone is disadvantaged if they are rendered less able to live a 'normal' kind of life. A poor epileptic will be disadvantaged by the driving ban, being unable to get around, although the rich epileptic who can afford the chauffeur, suffers no disadvantage. Banning someone from playing Russian roulette on the unwilling will not cause them disadvantage, in this sense, and so no compensation need be forthcoming. Nozick adds that compensation should be payable only for the actual disadvantage caused.

The connection between this and John Wayne is that John Wayne wants to defend himself, but this will violate people's procedural rights. We are, Nozick supposes, entitled to prohibit this activity, because of the risk of harm, but the principle of compensation says that we should compensate for disadvantages he suffers as a result. What disadvantages does he suffer? Prohibiting independents from engaging in self-help 'makes it impossible for [them] credibly to threaten to punish [those] who violate their rights, it makes them unable to protect themselves from harm and seriously disadvantages [them] in their daily activity and life' (110).

Yet the only consideration given in favour of the principle, aside from this result, is that it confirms our judgement that the poor epileptic should be compensated if we ban him from driving. But is our intuitive judgement here admissible evidence? The libertarian might say 'either the epileptic has a right to drive, or he does not. If he does not, then we can ban him from driving; if he does we must not interfere.' If we decide the epileptic has no right to drive[29] and ban him from doing so, we might feel very sorry for him, and choose to help, but this does not, in libertarian terms, show he has a right to compensation.

However, even if we do accept that the epileptic case is evidence for the principle, further disquiet is caused when we realize that if the Russian roulette player really was disadvantaged by the prohibition, as Nozick admits, the principle of compensation instructs us that compensation would be payable. Perhaps the Russian roulette player becomes crippled with depression – and therefore unable to lead a normal life – as a result of the prohibition. A consideration of further cases may convince us that the principle is mistaken. Suppose, for example, the reason why we ban someone from his or her especially risky driving is not epilepsy, but frequent over-indulgence in drink and drugs. As I understand it, the principle of compensation entails that here again there should be compensation for any disadvantage suffered by the prohibition. Few, I am sure, would be sympathetic to this claim. Our reasons for making the discriminations between the epileptic, the drunk driver, and the Russian roulette player probably rest not simply on the principle of compensation, but on considerations of need, responsibility, and desert. We might wish to aid the epileptic because he is a victim of bad fortune – he is handicapped – whereas the drunk driver and Russian roulette player may well be responsible for their own problems. We will generally wish to determine the extent to which people have 'only themselves to blame' before deciding what sort of claim they have upon us for help. However, having excluded desert and need-based criteria of distribution from political philosophy, in favour of entitlement theory, these arguments are not obviously available to the libertarian. The principle of compensation cannot be relied upon to produce acceptable consequences, and should be discarded, or substantially modified.

I remarked earlier that Nozick's libertarian conceptual resources are too meagre to allow him to make the distinctions he requires. No purely rights-based considerations appear capable of discriminating between the epileptic driver and the drunk driver, or driving generally and playing Russian roulette on the unwilling. Some libertarian writers may, if forced to see this objection, advocate the prohibition of all risky action, even the driving of cars. Others may start to wonder whether there is not a place for the concepts of need and desert in political philosophy after all. But if this is admitted, as we shall see in the next chapter, the door is open to the extensive state. If we are to take need and desert into consideration in the distribution of resources, then it would seem that some central agency is necessary to ensure that goods are properly distributed.

The Minimal State

Even if we can be persuaded to accept the principle of compensation, it is worth remembering that people are only to be compensated for actual disadvantages suffered. Why the principle is formulated this way Nozick does not say. However, in consequence, if John Wayne can easily afford to pay for protection from the dominant agency he is not disadvantaged by the prohibition, and so he is entitled to no compensation. Others who are not so affluent must be compensated for the disadvantages they would suffer, minus the amount it would otherwise have cost them to provide protection services for themselves. In essence the dominant agency can offer them protection policies at a discount, and the discount, in each case, is to be calculated so that no one is disadvantaged by taking out the policy, but no one may be made better off either.

There is at least one evident defect in this interpretation of compensation and disadvantage. The minimal state, it is claimed, protects all, and the argument is that it offers protection as compensation for prohibiting private enforcement of justice. However, given that there need only be compensation for actual disadvantage suffered, the minimal state will offer, not general protection, but protection to some, cheap protection policies to others, and the opportunity to purchase full-price policies to others. Not quite the protection of all we were expecting.

Nevertheless, if our reservations can be met, we have arrived at a situation in which the dominant protection agency resembles a state in many ways. It is the only authority which reserves the right to approve procedures of justice, and it protects many, even some of those who do not choose to be protected. Apart from the fact that some wealthy independents may choose not to purchase protection policies, and so go unprotected, are there other differences between the agency and the state?

One difference is that it may not intervene in certain disputes. If two independents – John Wayne and Clint Eastwood – are in dispute, then, as Nozick notes, the agency has no business interfering in their battles, unless it feels its own clients are at risk. However, Nozick feels that any state must allow people to settle disputes privately if they prefer to (although few states do grant people this freedom). Nevertheless, Nozick is sympathetic enough to the ways in which the dominant agency differs from the state to refer to the agency as a 'state-like entity' rather than a state.

A final question is that of whether the agency is stable. Perhaps some members will defect, and then demand subsidized protection. Nozick could here liken this manoeuvre to extortion, and claim that it is void under the terms of 'unproductive exchange'.

No one, claims Nozick, may legitimately threaten to do something merely in order to be paid for not doing it. However, this is not Nozick's argument against those considering defection. He points out that the subsidy will not necessarily be large, and that independents will have to look out for themselves in disputes with other independents, and so it is probably not worth defecting. Therefore the situation will be stable enough.

Has Nozick justified the state against the natural rights anarchist? The justification, we have seen, will be made in two stages. The first shows that the state is such that it is rational to consent to it. This will justify the state to all but those who, for good or bad reasons, prefer anarchy. Nozick's discussion of even the best realistic state of nature may work very well to persuade the rest of us. The second stage is to show that even those who object to the state's existence have the moral duty to comply with, and the right to receive the protection of, the state, at least on matters of the administration of justice. The general outline of Nozick's solution – prohibition and compensation – is without doubt ingenious, and a genuine contribution to the topic of political obligation. However, it is also apparent that Nozick's particular version of this general type of argument fails. We can summarize our primary objections by way of a dilemma. Does John Wayne's right to punish offenders clash with the procedural rights of the accused or not? If not – if we view the right to punish as already limited by procedural rights – then there is nothing for which compensation needs be paid, and so we have no reason to progress beyond the ultra-minimal state. But if there is a clash, then why should John Wayne's rights always give way? And even if this can be explained, the claim that compensation is payable rests on the principle of compensation, which is not argued for, is not derived from other libertarian principles, and, in ignoring considerations of responsibility for plight, leads to unpalatable consequences. So Nozick's attempt to justify the state is brave, imaginative, but flawed. He has not justified the state, but he has added a new approach to the problem to the repertoire of standard arguments. It is a shame, although not wholly a surprise, that others have not taken up this line of defence, to see whether more can be made of it.

4

The Entitlement Theory of Justice

Rights, Distributive Justice, and the Minimal State

Whether or not we believe that the state is in need of justification, we cannot but be interested in the extent of its legitimate functions and proper powers. Nozick, as we have seen, defends the minimal state, which exists simply to enforce natural rights and administer justice by means of a police force and court procedure. These narrow functions determine its proper powers and anything beyond this exceeds its authority.

One activity of many modern states is to implement policies to bring about what is taken to be justice in the distribution of wealth and income held by its citizens, or at least, to lessen injustice. One possibly serious objection to the minimal state is that it would not be able to undertake any policies of this nature. Suppose, for example, it is presumed that in the just society each person has an equal share of resources. It is, of course, highly unlikely that this arrangement would come about by chance, so some central authority would appear necessary to bring about distributive justice. But if we agree that this is a proper function of the state we would at once have made it more than minimal: it would be doing more than protecting rights against assault, theft, and fraud for it would also be redistributing resources in the name of justice.

Nozick seems faced with a dilemma. Does he assert the legitimacy of the no-more-than minimal state, and ignore distributive justice, or does he accept the burden of providing for distributive justice and thus give up the idea that the minimal state is the most extensive state which can be justified? His answer is to point out a third alternative: to derive an account of distributive justice according to which justice can be realized even by the minimal state. This is the role of his entitlement theory of justice. If we accept this theory then, although the state might be needed to protect property rights against theft, it is not needed to make sure that everyone gets their rightful share of resources.

Putting matters this way, as Nozick does in his Preface, implies that the role of the entitlement theory is secondary: it is the answer to a problem caused by the minimal state. This appearance, however, is partly deceptive. It has often been noted that it is against the background of a theory of distributive justice, and in particular of private property rights, that the argument for the state takes place. For example, we saw that one of the problems exercising Nozick is that, if a state protects all, some people must be made to pay for the protection services supplied to those who cannot afford them. Nozick had to find a justification for this which did not infringe natural rights to property. For Nozick these natural private property rights, therefore, are more fundamental than the state, and would exist, he would claim, whether or not the state is justified.

Even though, in Nozick's view, the entitlement theory holds true in the state of nature, it also has an important role to play in the argument for the minimal state. We should bear in mind that what will convince as an argument for a particular conclusion depends in large part on what one's opponent is prepared to accept. Nozick will not have convinced the natural rights anarchist that the minimal state is justified, but the defence of the minimal state will be quite different against those who already accept that some or other form of state is justified. The argument, in short, is that the entitlement theory is true. If this is so, then, as we shall see, at least in economic matters, the only justified state is the minimal state. In particular those who initially believe that a more-than-minimal state is justified must answer the challenge of the entitlement theory of justice.

Within *Anarchy, State, and Utopia* we can discern three distinct defences of the state. First, we have already seen the defence based on the attempted refutation of anarchism. Second, there is the defence at present under consideration, based on the entitlement theory of justice. Third, the minimal state can be recommended as a neutral framework within which one may design and live one's own utopia. The second project is probably Nozick's most important philosophical defence of the minimal state, for, after all, few finally accept the anarchist position, and utopians this century are thin on the ground (although if a convincing Utopia can be described perhaps we would see a resurgence of utopianism). Nozick's real opponents are those – conservative, liberal, or socialist – who believe there is reason to adopt a more than minimal state. In the end everything rests on the entitlement theory.

Theories of Justice: End-States, Patterns, and History

Before presenting the entitlement theory in detail, we might try to become clearer about what it is a theory of, and what its competitors are. We have already seen that we are dealing with the issue of distributive or economic justice: is a particular set of economic holdings among members of society just or unjust? As Nozick mentions, writers on this subject often present various wealth and income figures – the top x per cent own y per cent of society's wealth, and so on – and invite us to judge whether or not this is a just situation.[1] Different theories will give different answers, and, of course, some theorists, including Nozick, would argue that such bare statistics do not give us sufficient information to assess the matter at all. A principle utilized in order to make a judgement in such a case will be a principle of distributive justice: part of a theory of justice.

A great many views of economic or distributive justice are possible. Some theorists claim that goods should be shared equally, or, relatedly, that each person should be allocated goods entirely on the basis of need. Others have claimed that only labour may rightfully confer title to goods, or have appealed to various other desert-based criteria, such as effort, moral merit, or abstinence. John Rawls has argued that the economy should be arranged so that the worst off should be as well off as possible.[2] Thus, he argues, inequalities are permissible, but only if all benefit. It is clear that anyone who advocates any one of these theories must tacitly approve of a more than minimal state which diverts resources by taxation or other means to those who, according to the theory, may justly possess them.

Theories of justice, then, address what is commonly known as the problem of distributive justice: how the goods of our society should be justly distributed. However, Nozick notes that this way of putting the problem is not 'neutral'. That is to say, to talk about distributive justice seems to presuppose that resources exist in a big 'social pot' waiting to be justly allocated by some central authority. But there is no pot, only people and associations of people, the natural world, and what people produce. Thus we cannot treat the production of goods and their proper distribution as separate matters. What people get is partly a consequence of what they produce, and what they produce is largely a consequence of what they expect to get.

We can, of course, ask whether current holdings of property are just, and whether justice requires us to transfer some resources from one person to another, but if we continue to talk about distributive justice we will tend to think in terms of the 'social pot' and so blind ourselves to certain theories of justice. In particular we may overlook the very theory which Nozick recommends. Nozick's case is that economic justice can be achieved without recourse to any central distribution process, and thus can be achieved by the minimal state. Rather than 'distributive justice', he prefers to name the area of discussion, more neutrally, 'justice in holdings'. The entitlement theory, then, is one theory of justice, which addresses the issue of justice in holdings.[3]

In order to make it clear that his own theory is a radical alternative to its competitors, Nozick makes some important distinctions between types of theories of justice in holdings. First he introduces the idea of a *current-time slice* or *end-state* principle, of which, he claims, utilitarianism is an example. The essential feature of such accounts of justice is that they assess a distribution by attending only to its structure, and so it may be possible to substitute one arrangement for another without leading to injustice. It may be, for example, that A having 10 and B having 5 gives the same utility as A having 5 and B having 10. If so, then which distribution we choose will be a matter of indifference and no injustice would be involved in choosing one of these distributions rather than the other, or in moving from one of them to the other (assuming that the mere fact of the change does not generate any utility loss).

This type of view contrasts with what Nozick calls *historical* theories of justice which take account of past actions or circumstances. 'Each according to their contribution' is one such historical view in this sense. To tell whether a distribution is just we need to know not only how the distribution is structured, but whether, in fact, it corresponds to historically relevant features of people. Nozick divides historical principles into two classes: the patterned and the unpatterened. Patterned theories are those according to which the just distribution is to be determined by some 'natural dimension', or sum, or ordering of dimensions: each according to their labour, need, merit, etc.[4] Nozick suggests that 'To think that the task of a theory of distributive justice is to fill in the blank in "to each according to his ———" is to be predisposed to search for a pattern' (159–60). Not unreasonably, he claims that 'almost every suggested principle of distributive justice is patterned' (156).[5] By contrast, Nozick claims that his historical entitlement theory is not patterned.

The Entitlement Theory

What would an unpatterned historical theory be like? Typically, it will concentrate on ways of coming to hold property, rather than specify a pattern to which distributions must conform. That is, it will specify a procedure or set of procedures which must be followed if an acquisition of property is to be justified: your holding of property is justified if and only if you came to hold it by the correct procedure.

If the world were wholly just, claims Nozick:

> the following inductive definition would exhaustively cover the subject of justice in holdings.
>
> 1 A person who acquires a holding in accordance with the principle of justice in acquisition is entitled to that holding.
> 2 A person who acquires a holding in accordance with the principle of justice in transfer, from someone else entitled to that holding, is entitled to the holding.
> 3 No one is entitled to a holding except by (repeated) applications of 1 and 2. (151)

In thinking about private property rights it is easy to forget that there must have been a time when a particular piece of property first came into the private ownership of one person. How is it anyone can come to own anything? One answer is that people make things, and if they make something they become the justified owner of it. But it is not that simple. No one can make something out of nothing. A pot is made out of clay, a chair out of wood. How can people come to own the materials out of which they make other things? This line of thought becomes increasingly disturbing when one realizes that if not everything, then most things now in private ownership are either made out of things that were once unowned, or are made out of things descended from what was once unowned. Even if I own the tree from which I made this chair, probably I did not own the seed from which the tree grew, or the tree from which that seed came.

A principle of *justice in acquisition* tells us how things can change status from the unowned to the owned, and a principle of *justice in transfer* explains how goods, already justly owned, can be transferred to others. The essential core of Nozick's principle of justice in transfer is that a transfer is just if and only if it is voluntary. However given that the world is not wholly just, and people sometimes acquire goods by force or fraud, and so on, a principle of *justice in rectification* is also needed, to repair the effects of past injustices.

So the essence of Nozick's position is that the justice of one's holding of a particular item of property depends entirely on how it came into one's possession. If it was justly acquired, then it is justly held. 'A distribution is just if it arises from another just distribution by legitimate means' (151). It is easy to see why the entitlement theory is described as historical, and as it is a theory which puts procedures prior to any patterns which may or may not form, clearly it appears unpatterned, (although later in this chapter we will investigate a claim that there is reason to doubt this appearance).

The entitlement theory is not completely stated until we are told the precise content of Nozick's principles of justice in acquisition, transfer, and rectification, and so we should expect a detailed statement and justification of Nozick's versions of these principles. But again at a crucial point, we are offered nothing like this, for Nozick is content to present what he calls an 'outline' of the theory, a practice defended in the preface by pointing out that 'There is room for words on subjects other than last words' (xii).

Liberty and Patterns

Although, in a sense, the principle of justice in acquisition is the most fundamental part of the entitlement theory, it is the principle of justice in transfer which immediately promises the most far-reaching consequences. For Nozick suggests that it is 'not clear' how others can reject the entitlement theory of justice, and this extraordinary claim is based on the principle of justice in transfer. Bearing in mind how many political philosophers, at one time or another, have implicitly rejected the entitlement theory by adopting patterned conceptions of justice, Nozick's claim appears radical indeed. But the argument is very simple. It is that 'liberty upsets patterns'. A proper regard for liberty forces upon us Nozick's principle of justice in transfer – a transfer is just if and only if it is voluntary – but if we accept this it can be demonstrated that no patterned theory is acceptable. This leaves the entitlement theory as the only candidate still standing.

Nozick's demonstration relies upon an expanded version of Hume's famous argument that liberty and equality are not compatible:

> Render possessions ever so equal, men's different degrees of art, care, and industry will immediately break that equality.... The most rigorous inquisition too is requisite to watch every inequality on its first appearance; and the most severe jurisdiction to punish and redress it.[6]

Nozick's notorious 'Wilt Chamberlain' example generalizes the point to demonstrate that liberty – freedom of transfer – rules out not only equality but all patterned and end-state theories. Suppose that 'your favourite' pattern, whatever it is, is realized, and let us call that distribution of goods D1. Now suppose that

> Wilt Chamberlain is greatly in demand by basketball teams, being a great gate attraction ... [and] signs the following sort of contract with a team: In each home game twenty-five cents from the price of each ticket of admission goes to him.... Let us suppose that in one season one million persons attend his home games, and Wilt Chamberlain ends up with $250,000, a much larger sum than the average income and larger even than anyone else has. Is he entitled to this income? Is this new distribution D2 unjust? (161)

Voluntary transfers, so it appears, can upset any pattern, transforming it into a new distribution. Nozick's first point, then, is that voluntary exchange upsets patterns. But is this new distribution D2 just? Nozick's second claim is that it is. If D1 was just, and people voluntarily moved from it to D2, then D2 surely also is just. So, Nozick argues, we must admit that there can exist a just distribution not in accordance with the original pattern. But if we admit this, then we have abandoned a patterned conception of justice. Our only alternative is to refuse to admit that D2 is just, and decide to enforce D1, even though it is threatened by voluntary transfers. But how could we do this? Nozick's third, and most important point against patterned and end-state theories is that if voluntary actions will disrupt a distribution, then the only way of maintaining that distribution will involve preventing or otherwise nullifying those voluntary actions, and this will be to interfere with people's liberty. To maintain D1 we might either ban any transfer which threatens the pattern, or we might periodically redistribute resources so as to reinstate the pattern. (Although, as Nozick asks, how often should we redistribute? Why not have immediate confiscation?) But in any case we would need, as Hume said, to combine 'rigorous inquisition' with 'severe jurisdiction': watching out for and remedying the effects of any breach or potential breach of the pattern. This, Nozick claims, constitutes a continuous interference with people's lives, and hence a serious and unacceptable infringement of liberty.

Certainly, between them Hume and Nozick paint a dismal picture of the intrusiveness of a pattern-enforcing society, a picture reinforced by a claim made by the nineteenth-century French statesman Adolphe Thiers, who argued that 'A primary concern of socialist government will be to prevent men from saving and automatically becoming capitalists: every citizen will have to submit to examinations as intimate as those given to workers in the Mexican diamond mines.'[7] Nozick's argument for the entitlement theory is, in sum, that it is the only theory which respects liberty, allowing people to accumulate or transfer their justly held resources however they choose.

Is it true that upholding a pattern violates liberty, and if so is this a sufficient refutation of all patterned theories? This simple example, which many commentators see as the most important argument in Nozick's book, has been taken as a severe test by almost all subsequent writers on distributive justice. Part of the standard repertoire of any such theorist is to provide a response in order to show how the entitlement theory may be rejected. Hence there are literally dozens of discussions of Wilt Chamberlain in the literature, and here I have space only to consider those which, for various reasons, are most instructive.

One common immediate response is that Nozick's description of his example biases matters in his own favour. Many egalitarians advocate a far more radical transformation of society than that in which, in effect, we have capitalism with equal money. Some argue, for example, that ideally money should be abolished and there should be a central distribution of needed resources. 'Of course', it might be said, 'given capitalist trading institutions, patterns will be upset, but this is simply a reason for thinking that the just society will not contain those institutions.' A society without money might be thought to be poorly represented by 'patterned' conceptions of justice.

Nozick, however, has anticipated this objection. His reply is that even in socialist money-free society, people might want to exchange goods and services with each other, and thereby severe inequalities may develop:

> Notice also that small factories would spring up in a socialist society, unless forbidden. I melt down some of my personal possessions (under D1) and build a machine out of the material. I offer you, and others, a philosophy lecture once a week in exchange for your cranking the handle on my machine, whose products I exchange for yet other things, and so on. . . . The socialist society would have to forbid capitalist acts between consenting adults (162–3).

Thus, we must concede, nothing rests on Nozick's assumption that distribution is to be made in terms of money. If goods are to be held at all, even if allocated for consumption purposes only, then voluntary transfers are likely to upset the original distribution. This will be true for money and non-money economies alike. Nozick's three essential claims remain: first, voluntary transfers will upset patterns; second, if D1 was just, and people voluntarily moved from it to D2, surely D2 is just too; and third, enforcing a pattern requires an unacceptable violation of people's liberty.

The Disruption of Patterns

But is it true that patterns will be disrupted by voluntary transactions? One response is that patterns are not merely arbitrary; they would be brought about for a reason. In some cases people might be motivated by those reasons to attempt to maintain the pattern, even if they know they could destroy it through greed or lack of care. Suppose a society has fought long and hard for 'non-money socialism'. Individuals may well see ways of improving their particular share through voluntary transactions, but nevertheless restrain from taking them as they do not wish to disrupt equality.

Nozick replies 'This presupposes unrealistically (1) that all will most want to maintain the pattern ... (2) that each can gather enough information about his own actions and the ongoing activities of others to discover which of his actions will upset the pattern, and (3) that diverse and far-flung persons can coordinate their actions to dovetail into the pattern' (163). Is it unrealistic to assent to (1), or a slightly weaker view (1'): that the overwhelming majority will most want to maintain the pattern? It has been argued that this claim, and its denial, rests on a conception of human nature, and as Nozick has not argued for a conception from which it follows that (1) is unrealistic, Nozick has no warrant to make the claim.[8] Nozick, of course, would dispute that he has the burden of proof here, and one might think that the evidence of history is on Nozick's side. We have no evidence that people have ever, on a large scale, been sufficiently concerned about maintaining a pattern that they would strongly be motivated to do so even in the absence of coercion. Thus it is Nozick's opponent who has to establish a controversial conception of human nature to show that Nozick is wrong. What about assumptions (2) and (3)? These, it has been said, are 'red herrings. At most they are preconditions of realising [patterned] justice *perfectly*.'[9] The point here is ·that even if lack of information and imperfect coordination lead to deviations from the pattern, these would tend to be temporary – though possibly numerous and serious – aberrations rather than cumulative long term difficulties, for if people are motivated to keep the pattern, then they would do their best to correct any discrepancies which occur. Thus Nozick must concede that it is possible a pattern may remain reasonably stable even given voluntary transactions. Nevertheless, he might claim with justification, only in the most exceptional circumstances will this happen, and if society is at all divided on the question of whether D1 is the correct pattern it will not be long before D1 is left behind.

Voluntary Transfer

Thus we come to the second claim: if D1 was just, and people voluntarily moved from it to D2, then surely D2 is also just. This may strike one as an obvious truth, although there is reason to be careful here. Nozick claims that 'whatever arises from a just situation by just steps is itself just', (151) and this may well seem self-evident. However the claim under consideration is that 'whatever arises from a just situation by *voluntary* steps is just'. Thus to make his case Nozick needs to argue that if a transaction is voluntary, then it is just: that is, voluntariness is sufficient for justice. A different claim, also implied by Nozick, is that voluntariness is necessary for justice: a transaction is just *only if* it is voluntary. Combined, these claims amount to the essential core of Nozick's principle of justice in transfer: a transfer is just if and only if it is voluntary.[10]

Let us concentrate, for the moment, on the sufficiency claim: is every voluntary transaction just? Stated like this it might seem that there can be little to question. If both sides agree to a transfer then how can it be faulted? What harm would it do? Nozick's principle of justice in transfer has great intuitive appeal. But can things be so simple?

One first point is that it may not be easy to tell when a transaction is voluntary. Certainly the form of words used cannot be decisive. Consider the following: 'Your money or your life!', 'Here, please take my money.' In other words, we want to be able to distinguish between a free and a forced exchange, and the claim under consideration at the moment is, in effect, that every free exchange is legitimate. The distinction between free and forced exchange is not simply a fussy matter of detail, for it connects with an important question of the justice of capitalist society: are workers forced to work for capitalists? If they are not forced, then, they can have no complaint against capitalism, according to entitlement theory. If, on the other hand, they are forced, then for a libertarian the position is extremely serious. Thus it is vital to answer this question.

The claim that workers are forced to work for capitalists rests, in part, on the observation that if they do not, they will starve. Whether or not this is true in the modern state, it may well be so in a libertarian society in which there is no guaranteed welfare provision. So if a person is faced with the choice of working for some capitalist or other, or starving, does this mean that he or she is forced to work, or does not work voluntarily?

Nozick suggests:

> Whether a person's actions are voluntary depends on what it is that limits his alternatives. If facts of nature do so, the actions are voluntary. (I may voluntarily walk to some place I would prefer to fly to unaided.) Other people's actions place limits on one's available opportunities. Whether this makes one's resulting action non-voluntary depends upon whether these others had the right to act as they did. (262)

Hence there are two necessary conditions to be fulfilled if, according to Nozick, one may count one's actions as non-voluntary. First, one's options must be restricted by actions of others, and second, these constraining actions must themselves violate rights. Nozick illustrates this with a fable. There are twenty-six men and twenty-six women, all wanting to marry monogamously. Suppose all are agreed that, on the basis of 'desirability as marriage partners' there is a defined ranking, and so the men are ranked from A to Z, and the women from A' to Z'. Naturally A and A' will voluntarily choose to marry, each preferring the other to anyone else. Although B would really prefer to marry A', this is not possible, and so B and B' will settle for each other. This will be replicated all down the ranking, leaving Z and Z' with the choice of marrying each other, or no one. Are Z and Z' forced to marry? According to Nozick, they marry voluntarily, for all those people who shaped their environment by their choices acted within their rights. The moral of this story is that if a worker is faced with the choice of working or starving, the choice to work is made voluntarily, provided all those whose actions affect the conditions of choice have acted without violating rights. Thus capitalism is not necessarily a regime of force. The highwayman, on the other hand, who threatens 'Your money or your life!' forces me to hand over my money, as he has no right to make this threat.

Nozick's analysis, then, allows him to add the necessary detail to his principle of justice in transfer to distinguish free from forced exchange. We should be aware, however, that Nozick's definition of 'force' is somewhat eccentric.[11] It has been pointed out that his account has the consequence that a criminal rightfully imprisoned is not forced to remain in jail. And miners, trapped underground by a rockfall, are not forced to remain where they are until they are rescued. Finally, suppose I am drowning and cannot swim: you pass by in your boat and offer to save me for £1m. Do you thereby force me to pay you £1m? Provided that you are not the cause of my plight Nozick must answer that I am not forced to pay this money, and if I do, it is perfectly just. Others might disagree, saying that such 'exploitative' contracts – where one takes great advantage of another's need – are also forced, or, if not, are still morally illegitimate.[12]

But even if Nozick's usage of the terms 'voluntary' and 'forced' does deviate from the norm, it might be thought that this is of no particular philosophical interest. However, in this case there is an important point at stake. Nozick's implicit claim that 'voluntariness suffices for justice' rests principally on the fact that it corresponds with what we find intuitively plausible. But when we look at the matter in detail, and discover how Nozick is using the term 'voluntary' we may find that if we read his claim as he intends us to, it no longer expresses our intuition. Of course we may still agree, on reflection, with Nozick, but the point, simply, is to be on guard.

Now, just as people must be protected from force, they must also be protected from fraud, an issue about which Nozick says very little. Fraud, typically, involves misrepresentation, and few would claim that a fraudulent contract is a just one. To accommodate this, two strategies seem open to us. The first is to argue that a fraudulent contract, although voluntary, is nevertheless not binding, owing to the special circumstances of fraud. The disadvantage with this is that once this move is made we can no longer claim that voluntariness suffices for justice, for we would have admitted a class of cases which are both voluntary and unjust. The alternative is to say that under conditions of fraud no transaction is voluntary. Perhaps we would argue, quite plausibly, that the fact someone has false beliefs makes consent involuntary or 'against the person's true will'. Thus fraud, or misrepresentation, vitiates consent.

This approach looks plausible, but what should we say about

cases of non-fraudulent mistake? If you agree to buy London Bridge only to find out, after contracts are signed, that the bridge you had in mind is really called 'Tower Bridge', is it just that you should be held to the contract? In other words, is *caveat emptor* a principle of justice? Or is it adopted simply for expedience, to prevent spurious claims in an area where evidence that a mistake had been made is so difficult to assess? The question Nozick must ask is this: is a transfer involving mistake voluntary?[13]

Indeed, we can relate this point to a claim made by a number of Nozick's critics, who feel that they have exposed a chink in Nozick's armour. If a mistake about the nature of a transaction can render it non-voluntary, what about a mistake about its consequences? Or to make essentially the same point in a different way, I may consent to a transfer under one description of that transfer, but another description may also apply to it, and had I known that, I would not have consented. Is my consent voluntary? Edward Quest[14] applies this to the Wilt Chamberlain example, pointing out that while I might choose to pay twenty-five cents of my money to Chamberlain, it does not follow that I choose to contribute to the move from D1 to D2, for I may not realize, for example, that I am contributing to what I regard as an unjust situation.[15]

Nozick would no doubt reply that what makes a fraudulent contract involuntary is not merely the presence of false beliefs, but that another person has implanted those beliefs in the victim, in order to entice him or her into making the contract. In the case of mistake, the error is one's own responsibility, and no one else's. Mistaken contracts are, in the relevant sense, voluntary. All that matters from a moral point of view, Nozick would claim, is what other people wrongfully make or induce you to do. What nature makes you do, or your own error induces you to do, leads to no claim of injustice. Undoubtedly Nozick's position here can be made coherent. The question is, once more, does it remain convincing?

These worries are based on controversy about when a transfer is voluntary. In some cases, however, it may simply be obvious that everyone concerned has acted in a voluntary fashion: suppose that a series of transfers involve no force, exploitation or fraud, and everyone is fully aware of all material facts and are not mistaken about any consequences. Suppose that this is true of the Wilt Chamberlain case in which we move by voluntary means from the just situation D1 to D2. Unless one is a dogmatic defender of a pattern, can there be any reason to object to D2 on grounds of justice? In other words, if D2 really does follow by voluntary steps from a just situation D1, can there be any good reason to object to D2?

One thing we might consider is the effect of the transfer on third parties. In our example, a great many people transferred resources to Wilt Chamberlain. Presumably, many more did not. Do these people have any reason to object to Chamberlain's accumulation? Nozick says 'third parties still have their legitimate shares; their shares are not changed' (161). So on what basis could they complain?

G. A. Cohen, however, argues that this last claim of Nozick

> is false, in one relevant sense. For a person's effective share depends on what he can do with what he has, and that depends not only on how much he has but on what others have and on how what others have is distributed. If it is distributed equally among them he will often be better placed than if some have especially large shares. Third parties, including the as yet unborn, therefore have an interest against the contract, which is not catered for.[16]

The point is, money is power, and the position of third parties can be adversely affected by the build-up of power in the hands of others. Of course, as Cohen, says, we are not talking about only Wilt Chamberlain's exceptional wealth, for what happens to Wilt will happen to many others in the society Nozick envisages. Thus a class of people will emerge who, for example, can raise house prices through speculative buying, and lower wages by forming cartels. Thus third parties can clearly be affected by Wilt Chamberlain-like transactions.

Nozick ingeniously points out that Wilt Chamberlain can do nothing that combinations of people could not do together under D1. At first sight this claim seems to ignore the co-ordination problems alluded to by Nozick in his discussion of the stability of patterns. However, in this case such problems can be solved, for example, by the creation of trusts, and fund trustees can speculate too. Yet this point can be taken as an argument against the concentration of resources in trust funds just as easily as a defence of Wilt Chamberlain. Indeed, when we consider the 'as yet unborn', and the accumulation and magnification of inequalities through bequest, over generations, we may decide that voluntary transfer can lead to substantial unfairness. Why should Wilt Chamberlain's great-great-grandchildren benefit from the compound interest on Wilt's success? As Hillel Steiner writes:

> That an individual's deserts should be determined by reference to his ancestor's delinquencies is a proposition which doubtless enjoys a degree of biblical authority, but its grounding in any entitlement conception of justice seems less obvious.[17]

Despite the problems raised, however, we should acknowledge that we must permit at least *some* voluntary transfers, unless, as Nozick repeatedly reminds us, we wish to prohibit 'gift-giving and other loving behaviour'. But we must remember that Nozick does little more than rely on the obviousness that voluntary transfers suffice for justice. And as we have surely seen, this principle, particularly as interpreted by Nozick in a way in which force and fraud are prohibited yet exploitation and mistaken contracts are allowed, is far from obvious. To point this out, of course, is hardly to refute Nozick's view, but I think that we must recognize that the principle is much more problematic than Nozick suggests.

Justice in transfer is not simply a matter of the agreement of the parties making the transfer. Aside from the point that parties might not have agreed had they appreciated all the consequences of their trade, the effects of an exchange on third parties, and future generations, need also to be considered. The easy intuition that of course a transaction is just if it is voluntary, conflicts with the equally obvious thought that voluntary transfers can lead to a situation of manifest unfairness. Transfers require more supervision from the state than Nozick allows, perhaps even to the point where a pattern is thought desirable.

Patterns and Taxation

Objections to Nozick's theory might be brought to an end, however, if he could establish his third and most striking claim: that to enforce a pattern requires continuous and unacceptable intrusions into people's lives. Indeed we can see how this connects with the point that whatever follows by voluntary steps from a just situation is just. To enforce a pattern is to reject the view that a transfer is just if and only if it is voluntary. If we wish to maintain the pattern by banning certain voluntary transfers, then we are, in effect, denying that the voluntariness of a transaction suffices for its justice. If we maintain the pattern by compulsory redistribution, then we are denying that voluntariness is necessary for justice. If an effective defence of either banning certain transactions, or engaging in compulsory redistributive activity can be given, then Nozick's principle of justice in transfer is refuted. Conversely, to establish Nozick's principle of justice in transfer is to refute, it seems, all patterned conceptions of justice.[18]

Nozick's argument, then, is that to enforce a pattern restricts liberty. A certain picture of what it would be like to enforce a pattern is implied: constant surveillance to make sure no one gets too much or too little, and constant intrusions either to prohibit or to rectify the effects of pattern-breaking transactions. Life would be made a misery by the vigilance, and unpredictable, *ad hoc* interventions of the 'transaction police'.

But few have ever really advocated a pattern as rigid as Nozick suggests. Egalitarians rarely care about precise equalization of resources, but are concerned that some people live in terrible conditions while others have abundance, that some people have great economic control over others, or that gross inequalities destroy any sense of community. The remedy for all these ills will not necessarily need to be a strict pattern, although according to the egalitarian it is likely to involve a good deal of redistribution.

Such a redistribution scheme can be represented as a rather weak or loose pattern, and so one reply to Nozick admits that to enforce a weak pattern does restrict people's liberty in certain important ways, but it is a gross exaggeration to present the infringement as being as serious as Nozick maintains. It may be defensible to sacrifice some liberty to support other goals, and certain forms of pattern can be supported in this way. Thus one way to reject the entitlement theory is to argue that liberty is just one value among possibly many others.

Suppose, for example, that one advocated a Rawlsian approach to distributive justice: inequalities are permissible only in so far as they improve the position of the worst off. Rawls does not envisage that Nozickian 'constant interference' would be necessary to maintain such a pattern; this would be done by institutions of taxation and welfare benefits. Of course filling in a tax return is not a pleasant way of spending one's leisure time, and paying tax can be painful and cause resentment. But we must be careful here.

Nozick's argument is that to maintain a pattern by taxation requires constant interference with people's lives; it restricts one's liberty. This claim must be distinguished from the argument that taxation is the taking away of property which rightfully belongs to you. That may or may not be true, but it presupposes a view about private property rights. Nozick intends the argument that 'liberty upsets patterns' to be perfectly general, and not to be premissed upon a particular theory of property rights. His aim is to demonstrate even to his opponents that they must accept the entitlement theory, and the argument is that the means to maintain a pattern – taxation – involves serious interference with liberty.

We have all heard tax 'horror stories', where through no fault of their own, businesses have failed or lives have been made unbearable by the incompetence, delay, or 'honest mistake' of the taxation system. But Nozick's objection must be that even an ideally efficient tax system places unacceptable burdens on people's liberty. To what extent is one's liberty interfered with by income tax? At first sight the relevant considerations appear to have to do with the necessary intrusiveness of such a system: the bureaucracy one has to deal with and the invasion of privacy often associated with this.

Nozick's opponent may argue at this point that the burdens of the tax system – the intrusiveness – do indeed restrict one's liberty, but this is not really so bad as Nozick claims. It cannot realistically be represented as 'constant interference' in the sense to which Nozick appeals. So to enforce something like a Rawlsian pattern, by means of a tax and welfare system, relatively little damage will be done to liberty. In the trade-off of values, small losses of privacy and liberty are acceptable in exchange for a great deal of poverty alleviation. Thus engaging in redistribution from the rich to the poor, by means of taxation, appears not to involve a serious assault on liberty.

But Nozick maintains that taxation involves a grave infringement of liberty. Who is right? As a preliminary to settling this matter, it seems, one will have to engage in a philosophical examination of the concept of liberty: what exactly is it and what counts as its violation? Nozick's strategy, however, is to try to side-step the complex and often unrewarding debates about the nature of liberty by fastening on some clear cases. We do not need a philosophical analysis of the concept to know that forced labour, for example, involves an unacceptable violation of liberty. And income taxation, says Nozick, is on a par with forced labour. Taxation makes other people part owners of you.

Nozick's precise claim is that 'taxation of earnings is on a par with forced labour' (169).[19] The idea is that taxation is a way of forcing people to work for others: as Nozick puts it 'taking the earnings of *n* hours labour is like taking *n* hours from the person.' The Friedmans make a similar point, by suggesting a new national holiday, Personal Independence Day, to mark the point in the year 'when we stop working to pay the expenses of government . . . and start working to pay for the items we severally and individually choose in the light of our own needs and desires.'[20]

If we accept this line of reasoning, then, as Nozick argues, it is hard to see how anyone can defend taxation but oppose forcing the able, idle, unemployed to work for the benefit of the needy. Being opposed to forced labour, we should oppose taxation.[21] Further, the income taxation system unfairly discriminates against people with expensive tastes. Consider two people, one of whom enjoys movies, while the other obtains pleasure from watching sunsets. The movie fan will have to earn extra money to buy tickets, and will be taxed on these earnings, whereas the sunset lover gains happiness without expense. Thus we make those 'poor unfortunates' who must work for their pleasures, contribute to the needy, whereas those who get their pleasures for free are not so required. But why should we discriminate against those with expensive tastes by taxing them and thus making them work doubly hard to get what they want?

Of course, we might object to the claim that taxation is on a par with forced labour. It is not hard to spot some differences. Under a modern system of progressive taxation you will be taxed if you earn more than a certain amount of money, and how much you will be taxed depends in part on how much work you decide to do. Forced labour rarely includes the option of deciding how much labour to do. Further, most people have a measure of choice as to the nature of the activity at which they work, and who in particular employs them. These, too, are uncharacteristic of forced labour.[22]

Still, Nozick points out that one can imagine a gradation between forced labour and taxation. At the extreme you are forced to do one thing, then you have a choice between two things and so on, as we continue along the continuum to income taxation. However, it is not clear what Nozick believes such a gradation would show. Certainly it does not show that taxation is forced labour, no more than the existence of a biological continuum between amoebas and human beings would show that amoebas are human beings. Such a gradation seems only to prove that there is at least one property that the members of the continuum have in common. In the case of the continuum between forced labour and taxation, we have no reason to believe that this common property is grave loss of liberty, for as we travel along Nozick's continuum from forced labour to taxation, precisely what happens at each point is that more liberty is granted. If one can choose one's job, but not the hours one works, for example, one has more liberty than under a system of forced labour, but less than under a normal system of taxation. The sensible conclusion seems to be that although income taxation does limit liberty in important ways, and has some resemblance to forced labour, it is by no means as serious an infringement of liberty as forced labour.

But isn't the taxation system unfair to discriminate against those whose pleasures are expensive, and so need to work longer to obtain them? Perhaps it is, and, as Nozick suggests, this system is adapted only for administrative convenience. Or we might reply in the style of Rawls,[23] that although this would be unfair if tastes were as fixed as eye or skin colour, in fact tastes and pleasures are developed against a range of costs and expectations, so those with expensive tastes are likely to have formed and maintained those tastes knowing them to be expensive. One possible objection to this is that some people claim to be gripped by expensive tastes, which they would rather lose; indeed they are rather like expensive handicaps. However, few political philosophers have committed themselves to leaving the taxation system exactly as it is, and there certainly is room for discussion about which of all the possible schemes is the most fair.

In sum, certain types of pattern can be maintained by taxation and redistribution and although maintenance of the pattern may require significant losses of liberty and generate some unfairness, many welfare liberals would be prepared to tolerate this in order to advance other values, such as the reduction of undeserved poverty. Thus on these grounds, contrary to Nozick's claim, it may be possible to reject the entitlement conception, provided one also rejects Nozick's theory of rights.

Two Conceptions of Liberty

Those who find this reply to Nozick attractive make one important concession: enforcing even a weak pattern reduces liberty, although this is justified by the beneficial effects of the pattern. However, defenders of patterns may be right to be wary of granting even this much to Nozick, given the weight often given to the value of liberty. But can one enforce a pattern without reducing liberty? One extremely interesting argument is designed to show that enforcing a pattern does not necessarily reduce liberty, even if the pattern is enforced by *banning certain transactions*. At first sight this radical objection may appear to contradict itself, but Cheyney Ryan has presented an intriguing analogy to show that it does not.[24]

In universities, teaching positions are held by various people ostensibly according to certain 'patterned' criteria – desert, ability, qualifications, and so on. Thus, in some sense, we have a pattern of holdings. The idea that these positions should be freely transferable by gift or sale seems absurd. But it would be even more absurd to suppose that prohibiting people, say, from bequeathing their Professorships to members of their families, is a violation of their liberty. Although there is something we stop people from doing with their 'holdings', it is not plausible to construe this as reducing their liberty.

From this analogy Ryan draws the conclusion that what is to count as a liberty depends on a pre-existing account of what rights we have. As professors do not have the right to sell their jobs, it is no restriction on their liberty to stop them from doing this. Indeed the idea that liberty is premissed on pre-acknowledged rights is behind Locke's claim that the state of nature is not a state of licence but one of liberty. What he means is that in the state of nature people do not just do whatever they want, irrespective of the rights of others, but they respect those rights. Liberty is freedom to act within the moral law. It is a point Nozick acknowledges when he says 'My property rights in my knife allow me to leave it where I will, but not in your chest' (171). He would surely add, this restriction on what I can do is no restriction on my liberty.

This Lockean conception of liberty differs from what we might (perhaps inaccurately) call the Hobbesian conception, which, roughly, states that any restriction on what I am permitted to do –

the existence of any duties – is a restriction on my liberty. On this view my liberty is limited if I must refrain from putting my knife in your chest. For Nozick, however, my liberty is limited only if I am prevented by others from doing what I have a right to do. This, then, is another way of putting Nozick's view of forcing: just as, according to Nozick, you are only forced to do something if someone changes your feasible options in a way that violates your rights, your liberty is only restricted if someone stops you from doing what you have a right to do.

If, like Nozick and Ryan, we accept the Lockean analysis of liberty, then we do not know if something is to count as a restriction of my liberty until we know what rights I have. Consequently Ryan's argument has the effect of changing the locus of discussion from liberty to rights, which, on the Lockean conception must be prior to liberty. Clearly we do not give professors the right to give away or sell their posts, for we want to employ the best teachers and researchers. As they have no such right, it is no restriction of their liberty to prevent them from selling up. But what is the position regarding property holdings? Do they necessarily involve the right to transfer exactly as one wishes?

We must delve deeper into the notion of a property right. What is it to have a right to property? A number of writers have analysed the concept of ownership, and some important results have emerged.[25] First, there are many different rights a property owner may have over an object. The rights most relevant to our purposes include the rights to possess, to use, and to manage; the right to receive income, to modify, destroy, waste, or consume; to give it away, bequeath, or sell, and so on. The term 'full liberal ownership' is often used to refer to the conjunction of these rights, and to grant someone such ownership is to grant them all these rights. The second point, however, is that, as Nozick recognizes (282), it is possible – indeed common – to enjoy some of the rights but not others. Someone who rents a house has the right to possess and to use it, but not the right to sell it nor, usually, to modify it. Owners of the freehold of historic houses may have the right to sell and enjoy income, but no right to destroy their property. What this shows is that if someone has one of the rights it does not necessarily follow that they have them all. There is ownership less strong than full liberal ownership; indeed Ryan's professors had some ownership rights – what else was 'tenure'? – but far less than the full liberal catalogue.

We can apply this discussion to the Wilt Chamberlain example. Suppose we distribute holdings in accordance with pattern D1, and then prohibit people from transferring any resources by way of gift or exchange. According to Nozick this would interfere with people's liberty. But Nozick accepts the Lockean conception of liberty according to which your liberty is interfered with only if you are stopped from doing what you have a right to do. So the question is: do people have a right to transfer their D1 holdings? At first sight one might argue that if they are given the holdings then they have a right to do whatever they want with them. But this is too quick. One can be granted the right to possess and consume holdings without also having the right to transfer them. We might not like some of the consequences of this set of ownership rights, for it stops people doing some things they want to do, but this is not, in itself, a restriction on their liberty, on Nozick's view of liberty. D1 does not necessarily grant the right to transfer what one receives. Nozick challenged his opponent to imagine a favoured pattern, D1, and such an opponent might reply that under this pattern people hold resources, but not as full, liberal, property. We might build, for example, 'non-alienability' into the right to hold possessions under D1, or, as Nagel more appropriately suggests,[26] alienability subject to paying tax. People can be prohibited from making certain trades without this interfering with their liberty.

This argument, however elegant, sometimes has the feel of a 'trick'. Surely it is obvious that stopping people trading violates their liberty? So how can Ryan's argument be rebutted? There seem to be two possibilities. The first is to abandon the Lockean conception of liberty. The second is to argue that if people have holdings it is wrong to deny them the right to transfer these holdings. This latter course is Nozick's. What did we give people in pattern D1 resources for, he asks, except to dispose of how they like?

> Each of these persons *chose* to give twenty-five cents of their money to Chamberlain. They could have spent it on going to the movies, or on candy bars, or on copies of *Dissent* magazine, or of *Monthly Review*. But they all, at least one million of them, converged on giving it to Wilt Chamberlain in exchange for watching him play basketball. (161)

In other words, it could be urged, when we properly understand property holdings we will see that they do include the right to transfer. But here it is crucial to understand the structure of Nozick's argument. He has laid down a challenge to all non-entitlement theorists: to show how their favoured pattern is compatible with a proper regard for liberty. Cheyney Ryan has shown how, on the Lockean conception of liberty, this is possible: what needs to be done is to define a pattern of property holdings which are not construed as full liberal private property rights. To make the contrary assumption, that property rights have to be full liberal rights, is to beg the question against the patterned theorists. Of course, it is open to Nozick to find a defence for the view that property rights do include the right of unrestricted transfer, to find a philosophical foundation for his view of property rights. But once this move is made Nozick's argument has changed, and the burden of proof falls squarely on him. His claim that liberty upsets patterns will only hold, given the Lockean conception of liberty, if he can show that, when people have rights to possess and consume resources, then they also have the right to transfer these resources however they wish.

It may or may not be easy to show that there is a right to make some transfers, such as the giving of small gifts. Note, however, that Nozick needs to argue that not only are some transfers permissible, but that there is a right to transfer resources in whatever way one wishes. After all, a Rawlsian pattern will allow a great deal of room for transfers, although some will probably be prohibited, while others made compulsory by taxation. On the Lockean conception these retrictions will be liberty-violating only if they are rights-violating. To prove that liberty upsets patterns, Nozick must undertake the burden of proving that people do have the right to make whatever transfers they wish. Liberty is no longer fundamental.

This point requires emphasis. Given that a Lockean conception of liberty is premissed on a view about what rights we have, it would be circular for people holding a Lockean conception to defend that very set of rights by arguing that liberty requires them. The right to liberty is, on this view, purely formal. It is, in essence, merely the right to do what you have a right to do;[27] or to act within the moral law. No substantive theory of property can be derived from this right alone. An argument for rights to property must be made on a basis other than Lockean liberty.

Entitlement and Liberty

Suppose, seeing these difficulties, we reject the Lockean conception of liberty in favour of the Hobbesian conception in which any restriction on what you are allowed to do – the existence of any duties – is a restriction on your liberty. This would make it obviously true that banning transfers restricts your liberty, and it may well be that it is the Hobbesian conception we have in mind when we so easily agree with Nozick that banning transactions hampers liberty. Adopting the Hobbesian conception, however, has at least the unwelcome consequence for Nozick that if one accepts that all duties limit liberty, then this includes the duties of the moral law. Thus as my right to life prevents you from killing me, it restricts your liberty. The obvious conclusion to draw from this is that if a restriction to liberty exists, that, in itself, does not show that the restriction should be removed. Thus considerations of liberty appear to turn out to be far from decisive.

There may be a way, nevertheless, of making considerations of Hobbesian liberty paramount, and one which may appeal to the libertarian spirit. The idea is to accept the necessity of restrictions on liberty, but argue that the restrictions are justified in order to make the enjoyment of our most valuable liberties as secure as possible. That is, as Hobbes pointed out, the possession of unrestricted liberty makes the enjoyment of any liberty most uncertain. Even if I have the liberty to go where I please, this will be worthless if others have the liberty to rob or kill me as they please. The libertarian aim, then, is to create the maximum possible sphere of secure valuable liberty. Rights to person and property might be seen in this light. One is assigned a protected sphere of rights to one's body and property so that one may do what one likes with them, free from interference, provided one respects the similar rights of others. Thus rights to self-ownership and rights to property might be seen as maximizing individual secure liberty.

At this point, however, a new challenge is offered. We should not take it for granted that libertarian property rights best promote secure enjoyment of valuable liberty, for a distribution of property is also a distribution of Hobbesian liberty. An observation of Bentham puts the point well: 'How is property given? By restraining liberty; that is, by taking it away as far as is necessary for the purpose. How is your house made yours? By debarring every one else from the liberty of entering it without your leave.'[28] In other words, private property is *private*, and so to 'protect' a liberty by turning it into a right requires that we deny people the liberty of using the property of others, by giving them new duties of non-interference. Thus all property arrangements deny some liberty or other. If your house is yours, then I do not have the liberty to enter it without your permission. It remains to be seen which system of property maximizes the sphere of secure, valuable liberty.[29] Perhaps on the Hobbesian conception of liberty, liberty demands patterns.

So which set of property rights best promotes and least inter-feres with secure enjoyment of valued liberties? This question is, of course, extremely vague. How secure is secure? What do we mean by 'best promotes'? It may be that specifying these concepts in one precise way will lead to the recommendation of one set of property rights; specifying them another way will lead to a second. Indeed this problem is very similar to that of Chapter 2, where we saw the difficulty of defending a theory of rights on the basis that it provides the 'best opportunity' to lead a meaningful life.

To try to make some headway on this particular issue, let us consider the restrictions on liberty that are likely to be involved if we accept Nozick's entitlement theory of justice. Apart from Bentham's point that non-owners may not use the property of owners there is also the argument referred to earlier in this chapter that poor members of an entitlement society will have no legal means of survival but to work for its rich capitalists, who may also gain immense market power. On a Hobbesian view of liberty this is clearly a restriction on the liberty of the poor.

On the other hand there are some losses of Hobbesian liberty involved in enforcing a pattern; some of these we have already seen – Hume's 'rigorous inquisition' and 'severe jurisdiction' – and they will affect all members of a patterned society. One might contrast entitlement versus certain, perhaps egalitarian, patterned societies by saying that in the former a greater catalogue of liberties is available, but only the fortunate few can enjoy many of them, whereas in the latter a smaller selection of liberties is on offer, but many more people can actually exercise most of them.

This comparison between patterned socialism and entitlement capitalism is, of course, arguable. We might be sceptical about the project of counting liberties at all.[30] Or we might argue that, although, formally speaking, capitalism increases liberty, these increases are trivial compared to the sacrifices to genuine liberty that would be suffered. Suppose, for example, that as its next privatization measure, the British government decided to auction off the roads, allowing individual bidders to purchase any road, and then, if they wish, charge users a market price. In one sense this would increase my liberty, for now I am permitted to do something I was unable to do before: own a road. However, when faced with the inconveniences of having to pass through numerous toll gates when driving in to work, I am unlikely to think that the overall effect on my liberty is that it has been enhanced. Socialist joint ownership of roads would seem to enhance liberty rather than impede it. Conversely, Friedman and Hayek have both put the case that in a free market entitlement system, liberties are available to the vast majority which would be ruled out under any system where the state regulated property. The claim is that economic freedom is a necessary condition of political freedom, and one of Friedman's arguments is that certain exercises of political freedom – such as the advocation of radical change – are expensive.[31] Thus to enjoy such freedoms one must obtain surplus money, but in, say, an egalitarian patterned society, this would not be possible.

This case can, of course, be challenged. Macpherson accuses Friedman of assuming that money is a necessary condition for the command of resources, which is true under capitalism, but need not be so everywhere.[32] Clearly there is a great deal to be said on both sides here. So, which form of society 'best promotes' liberty? The question is ambiguous, and we need much more detail before we can even begin to supply an answer, but one thing we can say is that if liberty upsets patterns then it is also arguable that liberty upsets entitlement. In sum, little headway can be made by simple liberty-based arguments, despite their immense initial plausibility.

Rejecting the Entitlement Conception?

It would be as well to pause at this stage, to review the arguments so far. First we saw Nozick claim that it is not clear how the entitlement conception of justice could be rejected. His argument was based on three claims. First, that voluntary transfer will destroy patterns; second, that whatever follows from a just situation by voluntary steps is itself just; and third, that to enforce a pattern unacceptably violates liberty. The first of these points we broadly accepted but the second seemed over-simplistic. Nozick's own definition of voluntary transfers may allow transfers about which others may have doubts, but, more importantly, when we reflect upon the accumulated effect of voluntary transfers over the generations, many will think that, quite simply, voluntary transfer can lead to unfairness.

We also saw some responses to the claim that patterns unacceptably diminish liberty. First, liberty might be thought of as merely one value among others, and some sacrifice of liberty is perfectly acceptable in the pursuit of other valued goals. Second, and more radically, on Nozick's preferred conception of liberty, a restriction only infringes upon liberty if it infringes upon rights. Liberty is merely the right to do what you have a right to do. Thus to decide whether enforcing a pattern violates liberty we must examine whether the pattern includes the right freely to transfer goods in whatever way the holder wishes. But there is no reason to think that all patterns include this right. Thus enforcing a pattern need not restrict liberty at all. Finally, and most radically yet, on a Hobbesian conception of liberty, according to which one's liberty is restricted whenever there is something one is prohibited from doing, it is not clear that liberty demands private property rights rather than, say, socialist common property, or some other arrangement altogether. Thus there is even a case that liberty requires patterns.

We have, then, a number of responses to Nozick's challenge. Nothing yet is a refutation of the entitlement conception, but we have seen that Nozick cannot rely upon the appeal to liberty to prove his case. What he needs is hard argument that, first, people can form individual private property rights, and second, that in acquiring such property they also acquire the right to transfer, exchange, or bequeath it however they wish. It is to these issues we now turn.

Justice in Acquisition

How is it that someone may rightfully take some property from nature, and claim exclusive ownership of it? This must be a question of special seriousness for a libertarian. If a piece of land, for example, is unowned each of us is perfectly at liberty to walk across it, or use it in certain ways. Once taken into private ownership, however, all but the owner lose the liberty to use that land, at least without the owner's consent. Thus the acquisition of land by one person appears to deprive others of liberty.

This is more than simply another way of making Bentham's point that one person's private ownership prevents others from doing what they wish with that property. Appropriating property makes it illegitimate for people to do what they once were at liberty to do. That is to say, appropriating property inflicts new duties of non-interference upon people, imposing new obligations. Unless one insists that no one can appropriate property without the consent of all those affected by the appropriation, these obligations will often be imposed upon people without their consent. It is worth noting that this problem is the more serious the higher regard one gives to liberty. Those like the utilitarian who hold liberty as at best a secondary value need be little exercised.

By what procedures can one come to acquire property, and in particular land? The question has always raised strong passions. According to Rousseau, possession of property can, as a matter of simple fact, be traced back to what we might call the 'right of first claimant':

> The first man who, having enclosed a piece of land, thought of saying 'This is mine' and found people simple enough to believe him was the true founder of civil society. How many crimes, wars, murders; how much misery and horror the human race would have been spared if someone had pulled up the stakes and filled in the ditch and cried out to his fellow men: 'Beware of listening to this impostor. You are lost if you forget that the fruits of the earth belong to everyone and that the earth itself belongs to no-one.'[33]

Rousseau was making a historical claim not about right but of fact: this is how property came about. It is hard to read Rousseau as arguing that this procedure bestows legitimacy. Yet often it is supposed that possession does give rise to a right: the right of first occupant or claimant. We are fortunate that Voltaire's marginal comment on Rousseau's text, to be found in his personal copy of Rousseau's *Discourse*, has been preserved. An outraged Voltaire replied 'What! He who has planted sown and enclosed some land has no right to the fruit of his effort! ... Behold the philosophy of a beggar who would like the rich to be robbed by the poor.'[34]

Here Voltaire introduces a different idea: that effort or labour, rather than mere claiming, gives title. This argument, of course, was scarcely of Voltaire's own devising. It was Locke, in his *Second Treatise*, who had made famous the defence of the appropriation of property based on the labour of the appropriator.

Locke on Property

Like many who have subsequently considered the question of the justification of private property, Nozick begins his own reflections by examining Locke's defence of private property. Nozick's summary of Locke's argument is concise indeed: 'Locke views property in an unowned object as originating through someone mixing his labour with it' (174). This, in fact, is a fair gloss of part of Locke's argument in the *Second Treatise*. Locke argues that everyone has a property in their own labour, and so in removing something from its 'natural state' one 'mixes one's labour' with that thing. By doing this one makes its one's own property, provided one has left 'enough and as good for others', ('the Lockean proviso') and also that what one takes is not left to spoil. In this way, according to Locke, both the fruits of the earth, and the earth itself may come to be privately owned.[35].

A great deal of Locke's account of private property remains undiscussed by Nozick. Nevertheless we should note how very suitable to Nozick's position this portion of Locke's argument seems. As Nozick presents Locke, one becomes the owner of something previously unowned by 'inextricably mixing' something one already owns with it: one's labour. This argument seems to serve two vital purposes. First, it gives a reason why the person who has appropriated some item or other has a right to exclude others from it: it contains something which is already that person's, something from which that person already has the right to exclude others. Second, it shows why one's rights to private property are just as strong as rights to one's person or body: they are based on the something very like body rights, rights to control one's own labour.

There are, however, difficulties with Locke's argument. There is something very mysterious about the idea of 'mixing' my labour with anything, if this is to be taken as literally as Nozick takes

Locke. We might, for example, raise metaphysical questions about the possibility of mixing an activity with an object. Nozick, however, notes some further serious difficulties with Locke's account.

Nozick's first point is to raise the question of the extent of the object with which one mixes one's labour. Nozick's question 'If a private astronaut clears a place on Mars, has he mixed his labour with . . . the whole uninhabited universe, or just a particular plot' (174) is modern version of a criticism which must have occurred to many. Rousseau, for example, argued:

> When Nunez Balbao stood on the shore and took possession of the southern seas and of South America in the name of the crown of Castile, was that enough to dispossess all the inhabitants and to exclude all the other princes of the world? If so, such idle ceremonies would have had no end; and the Catholic King might without leaving his royal chamber have taken possession of the whole universe, only excepting afterwards those parts of his empire already belonging to other princes.[36]

Much more serious, and an objection which goes to the heart of Locke's argument as Nozick interprets it, is Nozick's second point. Locke, it seems, assumes that if I inextricably mix something I own – my labour – with something I do not own I thereby come to own that other thing. But, Nozick asks, why isn't this a way of losing what I owned, rather than gaining the other thing? One amusing example adroitly makes this point: 'If I own a can of tomato juice and spill it in the sea so that its molecules (made radioactive, so I can check this) mingle evenly throughout the sea, do I thereby come to own the sea, or have I foolishly dissipated my tomato juice?' (175).

Many suspect that Nozick, in his reconstruction of Locke, has not done justice to Locke's real view. Certainly Nozick's tomato juice example refutes Locke's argument if that argument is based on the premiss 'mixing what you own with what no-one owns gives you title to the unowned thing'. But is it right to see Locke's argument as based on this premiss? Might there not be something special about labour to which Locke appeals? One special feature, of course, is that in the normal course of things 'mixing your labour' with something makes it more valuable, or, at least, more useful. Locke does indeed attempt to add weight to his justification of the appropriation of property by appealing to this consideration. But Nozick asks: 'Why should one's entitlement extend to the whole object rather than just to the added value one's labour has produced?' Nozick goes on to comment, rather cryptically: 'No workable or coherent value-added property scheme has yet been devised, and any such scheme presumably would fall to objections (similar to those) that fell the theory of Henry George' (175).

This is, perhaps, an over-hasty dismissal of the view, even if, in the end, it cannot be sustained. Locke does have at least two things to say which may be construed as a reply to Nozick. First, he argues that in appropriating land one actually gives back to mankind more than one takes. Suppose that cultivated land is ten times as productive as uncultivated land. If you own no land you have to live from the produce of common, and presumably uncultivated, land. Suppose you need ten acres of uncultivated land to support yourself. But one acre of cultivated land would yield the same product. So if you appropriate an acre of land and cultivate it, in effect you are returning nine acres for the use of other people. Thus the point of the argument is not simply that in working on land you make it more valuable, and so come to own it. Rather the emphasis is that in taking land and making it more valuable you reduce the pressure on other resources, making them available for others.

Interesting though this argument may be, its achievements are somewhat limited. First, it assumes what can be denied: that land will or can be cultivated only if privately owned. Second, even if we allow this premiss, the argument can justify property only in land and only small holdings of it at that. You could not justify the appropriation of a second acre of land on the grounds that the appropriation of this gave back to mankind another nine acres, unless you were already using common land in addition to privately owned land.

Locke's second possible reply to the question of why making something more valuable gives one title to the whole thing, rather than just the additional value one puts on it is that, compared to the additional value added by the labour the original value of land is trivial. Locke goes as far as to claim that the usefulness of cultivated land is one thousand times as much as that of unculti-vated land. Thus it would be petty to insist that one should receive only the increment in value produced, and not the entire object.[37] Here, however, we should note that in appropriating land one may be depriving others of a necessary condition of creating value. If this is the case, it is not so petty to ask why exactly it should be that the land should pass to whoever is the first to labour upon it, even though the value of uncultivated land, considered from the point of view of its productivity alone, is minimal. To put the point another way, scarcity value should also be taken into account. (Although, of course, if the 'enough and as good' condition is met, there is no scarcity value.)[38]

Despite its promise Nozick does not seem to find exactly what it is he is looking for in Locke's argument. Part of the reason for this is that Nozick would have to look at more of Locke to find anything like a cogent defence of private property. But Locke's full argument has two disadvantages. First it relies on his theology, which Nozick does not endorse, and second, the consequences of the full Lockean account are far from libertarian.

We have already observed that Locke approaches political philosophy assuming that mankind is to be preserved as much as possible. A second assumption, for which Locke also claims biblical authority, is that the world is initially owned in common among human beings. Locke adds two further premisses in his defence of private property rights. First, that it is illegitimate to consume something unless one is its individual owner, and second, it is necessary to consume things in order to preserve oneself. From the combination of these premisses Locke is able to conclude that despite the fact that the whole earth is owned in common, it must be the case that there are justified ways of coming to own some private property. This argument at least opens the way for Locke to develop further defences of private property: given that there must be a way of appropriating property from the common store, what is it?

However, if one is to adopt Locke's first – preservation – premiss, it seems that further, decidedly non-libertarian, conclusions are likely. In particular it would seem to follow that, as Locke argues in the *First Treatise*, there is a duty to aid the poor out of one's surplus. Although this receives less emphasis in the *Second Treatise*, there is surely reason to believe that the right to charity is as firmly based as the right to private property.[39] And this, of course, is a conclusion which Nozick could not accept.

A further problem sometimes mentioned for Nozick in taking over Locke's arguments is that while Nozick views the world as naturally unowned Locke sees it as owned in common.[40] Thus there is a different emphasis to the problem of individual appropriation. For Locke the question appears to be one of how we should divide the common store. For Nozick the question is what entitles one person to exclude others from what once belonged to none of them.

Could one avoid the welfarist consequences of the 'preservation' principle and the reliance on theology by starting from the premiss that 'man has a right to survive', treating this either as self-evident, or as defensible on secular grounds? This position, which Nozick attributes to Ayn Rand, avoids the theology. However, precisely because it fails to avoid the welfarism (although Rand does not realize this) it cannot be used to provide a foundation for libertarian rights. Nozick puts the objection thus: 'The right to life is not a right to whatever one needs to live; other people may have rights to those things' (179). For example, if my ownership of x is granted by my right to survive, then if others need x to survive it would seem that they would have an equally good claim. This renders property rights conditional upon need, and gives them entirely the wrong type of character for Nozick. Thus he must reject the proposal to base property rights on a secular right to survive.

I think we have enough to conclude that it is not the case that Nozick can gain the support he needs from Locke.[41] Of course I do not mean to suggest that Nozick is under any illusions about this, but it does open up an issue which has caused bewilderment among Nozick's critics. Nozick apparently makes no attempt to clarify his position concerning the twin issues of the foundation of private property rights and his relation to Locke's writings on property. This omission has attracted some scathing criticism. It is clear from the outset that Nozick needs to provide a justification of private property rights, and the examination of his principle of justice in transfer has shown that the weight of the position falls upon his principle of justice in acquisition. So what is that principle? In *Anarchy, State, and Utopia* Nozick says 'We shall not formulate [it] here' (150). And indeed it is not formulated anywhere else by Nozick either. And if it is not formulated, what is there to defend? Concerning Nozick's relation to Locke, he discusses Locke on property under the guise of introducing 'an additional bit of complexity into the structure of the entitlement theory' (174). He briefly expounds Locke's views, makes the criticisms above discussed, and then comments that whether or not

Locke's theory can be defended against those criticisms, any adequate theory of justice in acquisition will contain a version of Locke's proviso that 'enough and as good' must be left for others.

We seem, at this point, to have three interpretive alternatives. First, to suppose that Nozick broadly accepts Locke's 'labour-mixing' defence of private property, and that, although he criticizes Locke's arguments, an amended Lockean position is, in his opinion, ultimately, acceptable. Second, that Nozick rejects Locke's argument, but concludes that a version of the Lockean proviso is a necessary condition for the justification of appropriation. On this interpretation no suggestion as to what are the sufficient conditions is made by Nozick. The third suggestion is to see Nozick taking and using the Lockean proviso as a necessary and sufficient condition for the justification of appropriation.

Each of these alternatives appears to confront grave difficulties. Concerning the first, Nozick makes no suggestions about how the labour-mixing argument can meet the objections, and, as I have tried to argue, that argument gets much of whatever force it has for Locke only when backed by Locke's theology. Not only does Nozick not want any part of that theology, as we have seen, but also it is fatal for libertarianism given its consequences regarding the duty of charity. The second interpretation is to claim, in effect, that Nozick has no theory of justice in acquisition. This, although astonishing, may be true, but, if so, then Nagel's striking description of Nozick's position as 'libertarianism without foundations' takes on further significance. The third alternative – that the Lockean proviso is a necessary and sufficient condition – does give Nozick a theory where he needs one, but in fairness to Nozick if this is his theory one would at least expect him to say so. In an attempt to make headway on this issue let us return to the Lockean proviso, and then examine what sort of role it can play in a theory of property.

The Lockean Proviso and the Nozickian Proviso

Locke argues, as we have seen, that one necessary condition for the justified appropriation of property is that 'enough and as good' should be left for others. Nozick remarks that the point of this is that no one's condition should be worsened by another's appropriation from the common store. If your appropriation makes me worse off, then I have good reason to object to it. The most straightforward interpretation of the Lockean proviso is that one may not appropriate something unless there is plenty left of the same sort of thing for others to appropriate too, if they wish. This was true of land once, we might think, but is no longer so. However, as Nozick acutely points out:

> There appears to be an argument for the conclusion that if the proviso no longer holds, then it cannot ever have held so as to yield permanent and inheritable property rights. Consider the first person Z for whom there is not enough and as good left to appropriate. The last person Y to appropriate left Z without his previous liberty to act on an object, and so worsened Z's situation. So Y's appropriation is not allowed under Locke's proviso. Therefore the next to last person X to appropriate left Y in a worse position, for X's act ended permissible appropriation. Therefore X's appropriation wasn't permissible. But then the appropriator two from last, W, ended permissible appropriation and so, since it worsened X's position, W's appropriation wasn't permissible. And so on back to the first person A to appropriate a permanent property right. (176)

We can call this the 'zipping back' argument.

Many have thought that allowing absolute rights to private property, when land is scarce, is bound to diminish the liberty of non-owners. Herbert Spencer, for example, observed that, for those who own no property, 'save by the permission of the lords of the soil, they can have no room for the soles of their feet'.[42] Nozick's nineteenth-century individualist predecessor, Benjamin Tucker, was equally concerned. Tucker did not believe in a natural right to property, nor approve of unlimited holdings of scarce goods, writing that 'It should be stated, however, that in the case of land, or of any other material the supply of which is so limited that all cannot hold it in unlimited quantities, Anarchism undertakes to protect no titles except such as are based on actual occupancy and use.'[43] Indeed, while Spencer argued for state control of land, Tucker contemplated that an anarchist voluntary authority might decide to limit holdings of land to ten acres per person, and this 'pattern', he implied, would be wholly consistent with individualist anarchist principles.

Unlike Tucker, Nozick wants to establish natural, unlimited, rights to property, even in the face of scarcity, and so it is imperative for him to reply to the 'zipping back' argument. His strategy is to distinguish a stringent and a weaker form of the Lockean proviso. So far we have assumed the stronger form. The weaker form states that there must be enough and as good left for other people to *use*, although not necessarily enough left to *appropriate*. Thus if there is not enough left for anyone to take, but enough left for them to use, then, on the weaker conception of the proviso, it is not violated.

At first sight, however, it is not clear that the advantages of adopting only the weaker form of the proviso are anything more than superficial. There is not now plenty of land for people to use. Does this, by the zipping back argument, make all holdings illegitimate? Furthermore, if we agree with Locke that privately owned land is more productive than common land, then we will run out of land to use in common before we will run out of land to appropriate, for Locke argues that land used in common, being uncultivated, can support fewer people than land taken into individual ownership.

In fact what allows Nozick to resist the 'zipping back' argument is the thought that even if there is not enough and as good land for another, there still may be, as a result of appropriation, other things which 'counterbalance the diminution in opportunity' (176). In other words there may arise new opportunities which compensate for the lost opportunity to appropriate, or, if we accept the weak form of the proviso, to use the land. Nozick points out how much better off people will be under a system of private property, for it

> Increases the social product by putting means of production in the hands of those who can use them most efficiently (profitably); experimentation is encouraged, because with separate persons controlling resources, there is no one person or small group whom someone with a new idea must convince to try it out; private property enables people to decide on the pattern and types of risks they wish to bear, leading to specialized types of risk bearing; private property protects future persons by leading some to hold back resources from current consumption for future markets; it provides alternate sources of employment for unpopular persons who don't have to convince any one person or small group to hire them, and so on. (177)

These advantages may compensate non-owners for lack of access to land.

We noted that according to Nozick the point of the Lockean proviso is to ensure that no one suffers as a result of another's appropriation. What Nozick has sought to do is to pare the proviso down to its point. That is, the Nozickian proviso simply says that appropriation is illegitimate if it worsens another's situation, all things considered.

Certain intended appropriations clearly fall foul of this proviso. No one may appropriate the only water hole in the desert, if others are dependent upon it, for lack of free access to water would certainly make these other people worse off than they would have been without that appropriation. The position is very different however if someone finds herself with all the remaining water only because, say, of all the well-owners she alone took special precautions to preserve it from evaporation. Then her holding does not violate the Nozickian proviso, for her possession does not make others worse off than if there had been no appropriation. Without her appropriation there would have been no water left at all (provided others would not have been just as careful with that well). On the other hand if it is purely accidental that she is the only one of with any water left – for example if an earthquake destroyed all the other wells – then her holding of the well does make others worse off and so the well reverts to unowned status. Applying the distinction between accidental and non-accidental will be difficult in practice, and will also lead to hard cases[44] although in outline the principle seems clear.

One consequence of the proviso, notes Nozick, is that it will also leave a 'shadow' over the principle of justice in transfer. If someone cannot appropriate all the water, then they cannot purchase it all from others either. This, then, is the qualification, referred to above, to the characterization of Nozick's principle of justice in transfer that 'a transfer is just if and only if it is voluntary.' Here, we can see, the voluntariness of a transfer is not quite sufficient for its justice, for it may violate the proviso if it leaves the entire stock of a scarce, life-supporting resource in the hands of just one person. However, in Nozick's view the proviso will have little role to play in any actually existing market economy. This is implicit in his discussion of a suggestion made by the Utopian Socialist Fourier that 'since the process of civilization had deprived the members of society of certain liberties (to gather, pasture, engage in the chase), a socially guaranteed minimum provision for persons was justified as compensation for the loss.' Nozick responds, 'This puts the point too strongly. This compensation would be due those persons, if any, for whom the process of civilization was a *net loss*, for whom the benefits of civilization did not counterbalance being deprived of these particular liberties' (n. 178–9). Nozick believes that the advantages of capitalism are such that those unable to appropriate land because it is all in private ownership are, nevertheless, likely to be better off than they would have been without the existence of individual private property rights. This is intended not as a utilitarian justification of property, but as a way of stating that existing property rights do not violate the Nozickian proviso.

Whether Nozick is right here is partly an empirical matter, and in a way it might be better for Nozick if he is wrong than if he is right. It is often thought an objection to the entitlement theory that the starving would have no right to food and would have to rely on the charity of others. It is often said, in justifiably outraged tones, that no theory of justice can have this consequence, and in this respect the consequences of Nozick's views seem far more harsh on the poor than those of Tucker and Locke. However Nozick's own position is more complex than this. We must address the question of why these people are starving. If it is because they have no access to land and are offered nothing to compensate for this lack, but they could have survived had there been no appropriation, then it appears that they do have a right to food. More precisely, their plight would require others to offer them compensating opportunities, or, if no such opportunities are offered, then this would show that the proviso is violated and so at least some claimed rights to property are illegitimate. Exactly whose rights would have to be modified is a question Nozick does not address; perhaps the burden falls on all. If so, then we have a libertarian case for general taxation in order to compensate those for whom civilization is a net loss. This consequence, explored by Gibbard[45] and Lyons[46] but little emphasized by Nozick, may moderate some of the anti-libertarian charges of 'inhumanity'. Nevertheless, the undeserving poor, whose plight is the consequence of their own fecklessness, would have no claim even on the surplus of others.

Some commentators have urged that once Nozick admits the Lockean proviso into his theory of justice, he can no longer maintain such a sharp distinction between his theory and patterned theory. For the proviso introduces a patterned element into the theory.[47] Certainly there is something to this point, for the justice of a holding, on Nozick's theory, is no longer defined purely in terms of the procedures undertaken in its acquisition. We also have to attend to the overall distribution of holdings resulting from that transaction. No doubt Nozick would reply that if any pattern is introduced by the proviso, it acts as a constraint upon transactions, rather than as a goal to be achieved, and this marks an important distinction. Nevertheless this concession would severely weaken Nozick's claim to have produced an entirely unpatterned theory.

Finally we must note an ambiguity or difficulty with the Nozickian proviso. It appears that it can be applied in two different ways, depending upon what is at issue. It is not clear whether Nozick himself is aware of this. Suppose we are concerned about the justification of private property in general. Then, as in the Fourier case, the question to ask is whether those who hold little or no private property are better or worse off than they would have been had there been no appropriation at all. However if we are questioning whether a particular appropriation is justified then we must ask whether that particular appropriation worsens anyone's condition, as in the 'desert water hole' case. Thus there may be cases where although another's particular appropriation would make someone worse off than he was before, still he is better off even after that appropriation than he would have been had there been no private property at all. An obvious example would be that of a farmer whose access to his land is made more difficult by the appropriation of the adjacent plot. Thus his situation is worsened by that appropriation, but not so badly that 'civilization becomes a net loss' for him. Nozick does not make explicit how he would wish to apply his proviso in this case, although it is reasonably clear that his intention is to apply the proviso in 'macro' fashion: that is, the farmer has no complaint because he too benefits from the property system which allows his neighbour to appropriate.

The Problem of Baselines

We have now seen some of the consequences of treating the Nozickian proviso as a necessary condition on appropriation. Should it also be treated as a sufficient condition: appropriation is justified if it makes no one worse off? Lyons[48] appears to assume that Nozick is to be read this way. Cohen suggests that *if* Nozick does have a theory of how legitimate, permanent, bequeathable property rights can be formed, it is based on the proviso which is to be seen as both necessary and sufficient condition for justified appropriation. But Cohen wishes to argue that as a sufficient condition the Nozickian proviso fails.

Cohen's argument is that, even if one agrees that a sufficient condition for justified appropriation is that it does not worsen the situation of others, Nozick is far too lax about what is to count as a worsening of another's situation. This is what Nozick calls the problem of the 'base line' for comparison. When we say 'worsen' the condition of others, we mean worsen in comparison to what? Nozick assumes that the relevant comparison is with the situation in which there is no appropriation at all. But why, Cohen asks, is that the relevant comparison?[49] Others seem equally appropriate. The point can best be made by considering a world which contains just two people, A and B. Suppose that in using the unowned land in this world A achieves a livelihood of m, and B of n. Then A appropriates all the land and offers B a job in a newly planned division of labour at a wage of $n+p$, where p is positive, and A retains $m+$ (positive) q. It would appear that this appropriation satisfies Nozick's proviso, for B's position is improved. But suppose that if B had appropriated the land she could, let us say, have done even better. Perhaps she could have offered A a wage of $m+q$, while keeping $n+2p$ for herself. In that case A's actual appropriation makes B worse off than she would have been under some other hypothetical feasible and legitimate arrangement. But why should this possibility, or the further possibility of socialist joint ownership, be ignored in assessing the justice of A's appropriation? We can make the point appear stronger by imagining that before A appropriated the land, B considered doing so but rejected the idea on the grounds that it would be unfair for one person to own all the land. Then A appropriates it and B is worse off than she would have been if she had appropriated it when she could. Has A's appropriation worsened B's situation or not?

Thus the problem of how to set the baseline for comparison is a difficult one, and Nozick gives us no reason to believe that his is the one we should accept. If we broaden the baseline so that appropriation is acceptable if and only if no one's condition is worsened in any way by appropriation, then Cohen concludes, 'a defensibly strong Lockean proviso will forbid the formation of full liberal private property. For there will always be some who would have been better off under an alternative dispensation which it would be arbitrary to exclude from consideration.'[50] Nozick's only apparent reply to this is to explain why his baseline claims priority, but this he fails to do.[51]

In Nozick's defence, it might be insisted that he nowhere says that the proviso is intended as a sufficient condition on appropriation, but only as a necessary condition. This, of course, is at best a partial reply, as its effect is to emphasize that Nozick does not provide even a statement of his vital principle of justice in acquisition. But is it even obvious that the Nozickian proviso is satisfactory as a necessary condition on appropriation? At first sight it seems so; how could appropriation be justified if it made another worse off than they would have been without any appropriation at all? But suppose, owing to his special talents, Arthur does extremely well under a system of no ownership, while everyone else has a miserable life. Suppose that if we instituted a scheme of property everyone would live fairly well, although less well than Arthur did before. So moving to this new scheme makes Arthur worse off. But it is far from obvious that this new scheme is illegitimate or unjust purely becaue it worsens one person's condition. Of course the case is arguable, but I raise it simply to show that there is room for scepticism about the adequacy of the proviso even as a necessary condition.

Finally we may remember that Nozick's claim that liberty upsets patterns turned out, given Nozick's Lockean conception of liberty, to be premissed upon a theory of property rights according to which the right to property includes the right to transfer. We saw, given Honore's analysis of property and Cheyney Ryan's argument, that this is not necessarily the case, for it is possible to have rights to possess and use, without also enjoying rights to transfer. So what is Nozick's argument? Does anything in his defence of private property rights lead us to conclude that these rights are transferable? As far as I can see, Nozick's only attempt to answer this is to try to make his claim true by something like definition. He writes: 'The central core of the notion of a property right in X . . . is the right to determine what shall be done with x' (171). But in the absence of further argument we have no reason to conclude that people have property rights in any sense that includes the right to transfer that property however they wish. So we must conclude that there is yet another gap in entitlement theory.

Whatever Nozick's intentions may be, I think we are bound to conclude that he presents nothing like an adequate theory of justice in acquisition, and so the entitlement theory remains substantially undefended. How embarrassing this gap should be for Nozick is an issue to which we shall return in the next chapter. But we must first look at the third component of the entitlement theory: the principle of justice in rectification.

Justice in Rectification

Nozick initially gives the impression that the issue of justice in rectification is a relatively minor matter of making a few adjustments here and there to remedy past wrongs. However, if Nozick's view is that we should remedy all wrongs which, according to entitlement theory, have occurred, then the prospect is mind-boggling. All state transfer payments are, on Nozick's view, illegitimate. The only legitimate forms of taxation are, according to Nozick, to fund defence, the police, and the administration of justice. Anyone who has ever received state health benefits, grants, bursaries, welfare payments, child benefit, rent support, and so on, has, according to libertarianism, received money which rightfully belongs to others. Furthermore, many present holdings can ultimately be traced back to conquest by force or fraud. Lyons takes these speculations further and even considers the question of whether, on Nozick's view, much of the United States should be returned to the American Indians.[52]

Nozick, in fact, is aware of some of the problems likely to be encountered in devising and applying such a principle. First, there is the question of the extent of the wrong committed, and the necessary reparation. Stephen Dedalus in Joyce's *Portrait of the Artist as a Young Man* asks whether, if a man steals a pound and makes a fortune, he must pay back that pound, or the entire fortune. Nozick must find an answer. Second, there is the question of whether it is ever right 'to let bygones be bygones'. That is, 'how far must one go in wiping clean the historical slate of injustices?' (152). One might think that if property rights are inviolable, as Nozick argues, then one must go all the way back. However, others may feel that the difficulties of doing this make some form of 'statute of limitations' desirable. For example, a 'popular libertarian' might agree with the entitlement theory, and hence argue that taxation for welfare purposes is illegitimate, yet feel all that needs to be done to bring the world to justice is to institute the minimal state now, *starting* as it were from present holdings. On this view, then, libertarianism starts tomorrow, and we take present possession of property for granted.

There is, of course, something very problematic about this attitude. Part of the libertarian position involves treating property rights as natural rights, and so as being as important as anything can be. On the libertarian view, the fact that an injustice is old, and, perhaps, difficult to prove, does not make it any less of an injustice. Nozick, to his credit, appreciates this, and implies that in all cases we should try to work out what would have happened had the injustice not taken place. If the present state of affairs does not correspond to this hypothetical description, then it should be made to correspond.

The consequences of applying the principle of rectification may be far-reaching indeed. What should Nozick say about the land claims of the American Indians? Or about the descendants of Black American slaves? Or about Marx's expropriated peasantry? In one short discussion devoted to these issues, Nozick comes close to taking back the anti-welfarism of libertarianism.

> These issues are very complex and are best left to a full treatment of the principle of rectification. In the absence of such a treatment applied to a particular society one *cannot* use the analysis and theory presented here to condemn any particular scheme of welfare payments, unless it is clear that no considerations of rectification of injustice could apply to justify it. Although to introduce socialism as the punishment for our sins would be to go too far, past injustices might be so great as to make necessary in the short run a more extensive state in order to rectify them. (231)

Indeed, Nozick notes that after a long period of injustice, and in the absence of detailed historical information, it may be appropriate to introduce as a rough rule of thumb something like this principle: 'organize society so as to maximize the position of whatever group ends up least well-off in the society' (231). That is to say, Nozick's theory of justice in rectification may, in certain cases, lead us to Rawls's Difference Principle!

Conclusion

So what has Nozick done to establish the entitlement theory? That theory consists of three principles. The first is the principle of justice in acquisition. As we have seen, Nozick does not make clear what his principle of acquisition is, and still less does he argue for it. One possibility is that he intends the 'weak Lockean proviso' to function as a necessary and sufficient condition for justified property acquisition: an appropriation is justified if and only if it makes no one worse off. This, we saw, founders on the problem of 'baselines': worse off than what? If it is not Nozick's intention to rest such weight on this proviso, then we are left with the fact that Nozick has no defence of the claim that legitimate rights to property can be formed. Given the weight of these rights in his theory, this omission is near incredible.

The principle of justice in transfer has, at its core, the doctrine that a transfer is just if and only if it is voluntary. It is this aspect of the entitlement theory that Nozick has in mind when he suggests that it is not clear how people can reject the entitlement theory. We have seen a number of strategies for resisting it. In essence, it is far from obvious that liberty is the only, or even most important, value, but even if it is, the argument that libertarian property rights are required by a respect for liberty is either question-begging, on a Lockean conception of liberty, or highly contestable, on a Hobbesian account.

The third principle is that of justice in rectification. In a sense, this is a matter of detail, for we need to know what rights we have under the other two principles before we can consider how to remedy injustices. If we find the other principles unsatisfactory, then the principle of justice in rectification is of relatively little importance.

We must conclude, I think, that although Nozick's entitlement theory has great initial plausibility, when his arguments are examined in detail it can be seen that Nozick has made little headway towards showing that we ought to accept that theory. Libertarian property rights remain substantially undefended.

5

Nozick and Political Philosophy

Looking over the arguments of the last three chapters, one might be led to entertain the illusion that there is little of real worth in Nozick's political philosophy. We started with his stark, and controversial, theory of rights, which, so far from being established, is barely defended, and appears to be wide open to criticism. Then we saw that Nozick's defence of the state, although ingenious, will fail to convince its intended target, the natural rights anarchist. Finally, Nozick's entitlement conception of justice seems left entirely without foundation. So what is there of merit in *Anarchy, State, and Utopia*?

We should, of course, remind ourselves that, in failing to demonstrate the truth of his views, Nozick is hardly alone in political philosophy. In fact, few have done more than Nozick to show that competing political philosophies are open to serious criticism, and a great deal of Nozick's importance lies in his waking others from their dogmatic slumbers. Later in this chapter we will return to the question of his positive achievement. Let us first look at Nozick as critic: of Rawls, of egalitarianism, and of Marx.

Nozick *contra* Rawls

Rawls argues that the just society should be regulated by two principles of justice. He states these principles thus:

1 Each person is to have an equal right to the most extensive total system of equal basic liberties compatible with a similar system of liberty for all.
2 Social and economic inequalities are to be arranged so that they are both:
  (a) to the greatest benefit of the least advantaged ...
  (b) attached to offices and positions open to all under conditions of fair equality of opportunity.[1]

The first principle – the 'Liberty Principle' – is said to take 'lexical priority' over the second principle, meaning that it must be satisfied before we even look at the issue of economic justice. In other words, there can be no justified reduction of people's basic liberty for the sake of greater economic well-being (provided that we are not in a condition of great scarcity). Principle 2a, which will be our primary concern here, is known as the 'Difference Principle'. Very briefly, Rawls's central argument is that if people were ignorant of those things that prejudiced them, directly or indirectly, in their own favour – their level of intelligence, social status, race, sex, conception of the good, and so on – they would choose these two principles to regulate their society. Thus the principles represent an impartial, and hence, fair, basis upon which to organize society.[2]

Nozick's main concern is with the fundamental philosophical grounds supporting the Difference Principle. For Rawls, the issue of justice arises by viewing society as a 'cooperative venture for mutual advantage'.[3] When people co-operate they undertake new duties, but also, in general, they will create new benefits, producing more than would have been possible without co-operation. Consider, for example, the productive advantages to be drawn from a system of division of labour and specialization of task. Co-operation, then, generates a surplus. The issue of distributive justice, Rawls suggests, is the question of the fair division of this social product, and of the burdens that produce it. What are the fair terms of co-operation? In Rawls's view the Difference Principle captures this idea. Inequalities are permissible, but only in so far as they serve to make the total product larger, as is likely to be the case if, for example, there is an incentive scheme. Thus inequalities may exist only when it is possible to make them in the interests of all. And so, argues Rawls, inequalities are justified only if they improve the condition of the worst-off group as much as possible.

Does the Difference Principle really represent fair terms of co-operation? Let us consider first the likely reactions of those members of the worst-off group in society. Apparently these people have every reason to be delighted with the Difference Principle, for they are to be made as well off as they possibly could be.[4] But consider the best-off group. It is highly likely that these people would be much better off under, say, the entitlement conception of justice, where they could accumulate without limit, rather than being constrained always to promote the interests of the worst off. Thus they may well resent the Difference Principle as quite unfair to them, objecting to this restriction in their earning power. Here, then, we have an asymmetry, for the worst off are happy, but the best off may feel unfairly treated. If the Difference Principle is supposed to be a fair division of the surplus generated by co-operation, then it appears to fail, for it is biased in favour of the worst off.

Rawls's main reply to this type of argument is to ask why it is that the well off would be able to achieve so much more under a different conception of justice. The answer is that those able to do better are those, in general, who are better endowed with 'social assets' – advantageous family and class background, and so on – or 'natural assets', such as strength, charm, skill, intelligence. But possession of social and natural assets is simply a matter of good fortune, and is 'arbitrary from the moral point of view'. Why should people expect to be able to achieve more material success than others just because they have superior assets? Certainly no one deserves these assets, so why should anyone think that they are entitled to benefit from them? Instead of viewing skills and intelligence as the individual property of those in whom they inhere, Rawls argues that we should regard them as common assets, from which all members of society should benefit. Thus the claim that restricting the earning power of the better endowed is unfair is without merit, for it assumes, falsely, that they are entitled to benefit from their undeserved social and natural assets. If we view people's abilities as communal property, then the Difference Principle will represent fair terms of co-operation, for inequalities are permissible if and only if they work out better for everyone. Otherwise, things should be shared equally.

Many people might accept that advantageous social positions are generally undeserved and unfair, but is it so clear that talents are undeserved? Some people work hard to develop their natural assets, while others let their abilities go to waste. Perhaps those who put in the effort to cultivate their abilities deserve at least some return on that effort. Rawls replies that even the preparedness to make an effort to develop one's abilities will be influenced by many factors – social status, parental support, other natural abilities – possession of which, too, is arbitrary from a moral point of view.[5] Hence the claim that some of those with natural assets deserve those assets cannot be defended on the grounds that those abilities have been developed, for having the capacity or opportunity to develop one's talents is itself an undeserved natural or social asset.

Nozick has what can be taken as three replies to this argument. First, this view of what one has, or fails to have, responsibility for, presents us with a diminished conception of a person, of a person who is not even responsible for trying, or omitting to try, to perform actions:

> This line of argument can succeed in blocking the introduction of a person's autonomous choices and actions (and their results) only by attributing *everything* noteworthy about the person to certain sorts of 'external' factors. So denigrating a person's autonomy and prime responsibility for his actions is a risky line to take for a theory that otherwise wishes to buttress the dignity and self-respect of autonomous beings. (214)[6]

This objection has inspired an important line of criticism of Rawls, most fully developed by Michael Sandel,[7] which accuses Rawls of basing his political philosophy on an untenable metaphysics of the self, a charge which continues to generate great debate.[8]

A related point, made by Sandel, is that if we discount positive desert claims on the basis of Rawls's argument, then we should also deny the negative desert claim that criminals deserve punishment for their crimes. It would seem to follow from Rawls's argument – apparently absurdly – that we should regard a 'criminal character' as a 'natural liability', perhaps augmented by negative social factors, and the costs of this should be spread out over the entire community, rather than falling on the criminal.[9]

Nozick's second reply to Rawls is to ask whether it really is so arbitrary from a moral point of view that people have the natural assets they do. Perhaps people do not deserve their traits, but, as we have seen, in order to be entitled to something it is not necessary that it is deserved. Thus, people may be entitled to their natural assets, even if these are undeserved. If this is so, possession is not, after all, morally arbitrary, and we have no warrant to try to wipe out 'the contingencies of social fortune'.

The third reply made by Nozick is that Rawls's Difference Principle violates the separateness of persons. It requires that we prevent the better endowed gaining extra material benefits for themselves unless this would also improve the position of the worst off. But this seems to be to using the better endowed as a resource for the less well endowed, sacrificing one person's welfare for the sake of another. If Rawls can be convicted on this score then the objection is particularly telling, for it is Rawls who argued that utilitarianism is seriously at fault for ignoring the separateness of persons. So, Nozick argues, Rawls fails by his own standards.

Whether Rawls can meet these criticisms is an interesting question. Further replies can be attempted to each of Nozick's objections. To the first, partly on Rawls's behalf, Scanlon has distinguished two senses to Rawls's claim that we should treat natural assets as common, not individual, property. We can best make the distinction by use of a familiar point from the theory of private property rights. It is common to distinguish the possession and enjoyment of an item of property from its full ownership, which allows one to receive a financial return on its sale and hire. Similarly we can distinguish one's right to identify with and enjoy one's natural assets and one's right to keep all the profit that can be made from them. Rawls denies that you are entitled to profit from your natural assets on the grounds that your possession of them is simply a matter of arbitrary good fortune. But to deny that you are entitled to profit from your natural assets does not entail that these assets are not properly yours, or part of you, there for you to identify with and enjoy. If you have worked hard to develop your skills, you certainly can 'claim credit' for this, for it is something you are responsible for. But this does not mean that you are entitled to all the financial return. In conclusion, then, there may be no need to attribute to Rawls a 'diminished conception of the person'.[10]

Nozick's second objection was that even if people do not deserve their natural assets they may still be entitled to them. We can grant this point, but ask why it is thought that people are entitled to their natural assets. To point out that desert is not necessary for entitlement is not in itself a reason for believing that people are entitled to their natural assets. What is the argument for this entitlement claim? Rawls's own attempt to undermine entitlement theory will be explained in the concluding section. Finally, we can grant that there is some justice to Nozick's third objection – the claim that Rawls is as guilty as the utilitarians in not taking seriously the separateness of persons. However, it is possible that Nozick wishes to read more into this idea than Rawls. Rawls's primary worry about utilitarianism is that it would, in certain circumstances, demand the further sacrifices of the poor for the sake of those who are already rich. The Difference Principle clearly avoids this.

Of course none of these debates need stop here, and Nozick's objections may be capable of yet further development. What is clear, however, is that Nozick has probed deeply into Rawls's assumptions, and has presented objections of fundamental importance. It is still a moot point whether Rawls's theory can recover from Nozick's criticism.

Nozick *contra* Equality

Quite clearly the main thrust of the entitlement conception of justice is opposed to egalitarianism. But this is not to say that Nozick favours inequality, for he is against the imposition of any patterned distribution of resources. It is likely – some would say certain – that in a libertarian society massive inequalities would develop, but if equality of wealth came about by chance or by voluntary co-operation this would be remarkable but unobjectionable. It would, however, be objectionable to bring about equality by 'social planning', via some central redistributional scheme, for this would violate people's entitlements to their property.

Many writers, however, have assumed that an unequal society is an unjust society; therefore if libertarianism leads to inequality it also leads to injustice. But why, Nozick asks, should we link equality of wealth and justice in holdings this way? What is the argument? One famous version comes from Bernard Williams who does not precisely conclude that people should receive an equal share of resources, but that vital goods should be allocated on the basis of need. This, of course, is one important variety of egalitarianism, and is, for example, one of the principles on which the British National Health Service is based. Indeed, Williams constructs his argument around the example of medical care. He begins with the thought that, 'leaving aside preventive medicine, the proper ground of distribution of medical care is ill health; this is a necessary truth.'[11] However, if one also has to pay to receive medical care, then this leads to the possibility that those who are poor and ill will not receive care. But if the proper ground of distribution is ill health then making people pay for medical care is irrational. Thus rationality requires the distribution of medical care on grounds of medical need.

According to Nozick, Williams's argument assumes that if an activity has an 'internal goal' (making people healthy in the case of medicine) then it is a necessary truth that the activity should be arranged so best to fulfil this internal goal. Supplying goods on the basis of need seems to be the way to satisfy this demand. But, Nozick points out, if it is a necessary truth that medical services should be supplied on the basis of medical need, should it not also be a necessary truth that barbering services should be supplied on the basis of barbering need? And 'need a gardener allocate his services to those lawns which need him most?' (234). This, surely, is absurd.[12]

Michael Walzer tries to reply to Nozick by arguing that it is not the 'internal goal' of medicine that makes appropriate its supply on the basis of need, but its 'social meaning'.[13] In our society, health is so important to us that our understanding is that it ought to be communally provided, and made available on the grounds of need. If good haircuts were seen as of overwhelming social importance, then it might be right to supply barbering services on the basis of need too. Given the way society is, however, no such provision need be made.

Nozick, of course, would be no more impressed by this variant of the argument. First of all, it remains to be shown that goods should be allocated in accordance with their social meanings. But more importantly, both Williams and Walzer appear to overlook the fact that if goods are to be provided, they must be provided by people. Why is it not up to the provider to decide on what grounds the good is to be supplied? To talk about 'proper grounds of distribution' suggests the 'big social pot' once more, and treats production and distribution as unconnected. But doctors, barbers, and gardeners go into their professions with their own goals in mind, and these goals will often be to make money to further other projects, noble or otherwise. Why should the 'internal goal' or 'social meaning' of a service take priority over the goals of people providing it? We have no argument that it should, and so, in the end, there is no argument here for equality.

Of course there are other defences of egalitarianism, and one common strain utilizes one or both of the notions of self-esteem and envy. On Nozick's understanding of envy, 'The envious person, if he cannot (also) possess a thing (talent, and so on) that someone else has, prefers that the other person not have it either' (239). Opponents of equality often suppose that the case for equality is fundamentally based on considerations of envy. If the poor cannot also have what the rich have, then no one should have it. This is why egalitarianism is sometimes disparaged as 'levelling down'. Nozick says that he finds it 'incomprehensible' how objections based on envy can be thought to involve claims of justice (162).

One obvious argument for the desirability of an envy-free society, not discussed by Nozick, is that a society containing a large class of envious people will be divided, unstable, and generate social unrest or even revolution. So in the common interest of peace, the sources of envy should be removed, and equality established. But steps other than the establishment of equality can be taken to reduce envy within a society. Joseph Heller reports that in 1646 'Amsterdam bakers of fancy cakes were prohibited from displaying overdecorated wares in their windows "lest they bring sadness to people too poor to buy them and stimulate covetous instincts to arise in their hearts".'[14] Furthermore, even if equality is desired to prevent social unrest, this seems not to be in itself a *moral* argument, but something more akin to extortion. To compel some people to give up or destroy their goods for no other reason than to stop others from rioting, may, on extreme occasions, have pragmatic justification, but hardly seems required by a concern for justice.

A more promising line of argument appears to be to connect equality with self-esteem. The argument might be that it is a good thing if all people esteem themselves, but developing a sense of self-esteem will be impossible for those who see themselves as socially inferior through the possession of a relatively small share of resources. Hence to develop the self-esteem of all, it is necessary to bring about material equality.

Nozick suggests that the weakness in this argument is that self-esteem depends not upon seeing oneself as equal to others, but upon seeing oneself as 'scoring' better than many or most others along some dimension one values. Self-esteem, Nozick argues, is essentially a comparative notion. In our society it would be a wonderful thing to be, in Trotsky's example, 'an Aristotle, a Goethe, or a Marx'. But if everyone achieved this standard little self-esteem would be generated by it. 'People do not gain self-esteem from their common human capacities by comparing them-selves to animals who lack them. ("I'm pretty good; I have an opposable thumb and can speak some language.")' (243). This fact, Nozick suggests, explains why some people are envious of others, for the existence of those who do better than oneself, along one's favoured dimension, threatens one's own self-esteem.

Nozick's idea that self-esteem depends on comparisons with others is, of course, controversial.[15] It does not always seem true that a secure sense of one's own worth depends upon thinking of oneself as better than others, although this may sometimes be the case. Self-esteem might also be fostered by knowing that one has the respect of those one respects, or by the thought that one is engaged in a worthwhile project, however large or small one's part. In neither of these latter cases does it seem important that one is measuring oneself against others. As Anthony Skillen remarks, 'A boat builder is happy if his boat has what a boat needs; he doesn't need a reserve army of incompetents to maintain his self-esteem.'[16]

However, at least to the extent that Nozick is right, then equalizing resources is neither necessary nor sufficient for develop-ing general self-esteem. Indeed, that project may be impossible, but as Nozick notes, the most promising route towards universal self-esteem may be to encourage the development of a plurality of dimensions, which different people may value to differing degrees. The hope would be that everyone may do at least reasonably well along a dimension valued at least by a reasonable number of other people. But theology and the world of children's books aside, this is only a hope.

Nozick *contra* Marx

Capitalism has, of course, attracted a great deal of radical criticism, and, as libertarianism is widely thought to lead to untrammelled capitalism,[17] then it seems likely to collect criticism of this type. Two of the most important criticisms of the capitalist market from within the Marxist tradition are that under capitalism workers are alienated, and that they are exploited by capitalists. Nozick seeks to show that neither of these objections can be sustained.

Nozick implicitly treats the problem of alienation through discussion of three charges central to the Marxist case. First, that capitalism fails to provide meaningful work; second, that it prevents 'workers control' over their own economic activity; and third, that it often does not allow workers a say in matters which affect them.

The point that under modern capitalism many people find themselves engaged in apparently meaningless tasks is well known, and well portrayed by movies such as Charlie Chaplin's *Modern Times* and Fritz Lang's *Metropolis*.[18] What meaningful work would be is less clear, but as Nozick notes, it is normally said to involve activity which exercises the individual's talents in some form of worthy enterprise, in which the individual understands his or her role. Meaningful work enhances the life of the individual, and provides fulfilment. The cost of capitalism, then, is said to be that a great many people are unable to exercise their skills and talent, to the detriment of their flourishing as individuals.

One reply to this argument, which Nozick makes in passing, is that it is not clear that the evils of meaningless work are specific to capitalism. Indeed, experience suggests that this is a by-product of any industrial society, capitalist or socialist. But Nozick's main claim is that the capitalist market by no means makes impossible the provision of meaningful work. If meaningful work is no less efficient, by market criteria, than meaningless work, it will be commonly available on the market. Otherwise, it will still be available, provided someone is prepared to pay its costs. That is, if workers really want meaningful work, then they can purchase it, by accepting lower wages. Thus we have essentially a question of the workers' priorities: meaningless work and high wages, or meaningful work and low wages.

While this reply seems perfectly consistent with free market theory, there are two respects in which it may be thought to be unsatisfactory. First it is a remarkable fact, although well known, that jobs which are most menial and dispiriting are often the least well paid. The reason for this is probably that there is simply a larger pool of workers available to do menial work. But this is enough to show that the trade-off between meaningful work and high wages does not exist, at least in some sectors of the economy.

Second, those who work to support themselves and their families may face a serious dilemma, for the cost of accepting low-paid meaningful work for oneself may be to inflict hardship upon one's family. Thus for many people this would not be considered a viable option.

Despite these replies, Nozick has raised a general point of great importance. Suppose, as seems likely, meaningful work is less efficient than deadeningly dull work, as efficiency is often a direct consequence of specialization and repetition of task. Suppose also that we decide to move to a society which contains only meaningful work. The consequence of this will be a reduced average standard of living, for society will be less productive. But can we presume that everyone would want to do meaningful work at the cost of a lower standard of living? The ideal solution – if it could be made to work – would seem to be Nozick's: those who want to do meaningful work do so, while those who want a higher standard of living take on the best paid work, whatever it is.

The second component in the 'alienation' objection to capitalism is that it does not allow workers control over their own economic activity. Although some firms do make some concessions to worker democracy, these are very limited, and hardly amount to workers' control. Thus a great deal of a worker's life is spent in following other people's orders, without the right to question, or even to discover the reason for those orders. But, Nozick suggests, if workers want to control their own destiny, why should they not start up their own co-operatives? In theory these should do very well in the market economy, for there will be no outside shareholders creaming off the profit, thus greatly reducing costs.[19] Nozick is not, however, optimistic about the prospects of long-term co-operative success, pointing out the economic problems likely to arise. Co-operatives have a tendency to favour average profits per worker to total profits, thus keeping enterprises smaller and less efficient than they might be. Further, co-operatives have no incentive to invest in long-term projects.[20] Nevertheless, in essence, similar issues arise here as in the case of meaningful work. If co-operative work is thought to be important, but less economically efficient than capitalist work, then co-operatives could start up, paying their members below market rates.

Could co-operatives raise the initial capital to start up? Nozick thinks that as long as they were thought to be able to flourish, they could get some sort of support in a market economy. 'And don't say that it is against the class interests of investors to support the growth of some enterprise that if successful would end or diminish the investment system. Investors are not so altruistic. They act in their personal and not in their class interests' (252–3). But, even if private investors would not come to the aid of co-operatives, what about the immense funds held by unions, and their pension schemes? It is, Nozick remarks, 'illuminating to consider why unions don't start new businesses' (253). We will return to this when we look at the issue of exploitation.

The final 'alienation' charge considered by Nozick is that under capitalism many people have no real say in the decisions that affect them. Under capitalism, Marx wrote, people become 'the playthings of alien forces'. One's livelihood could depend on the management decisions of the company for whom one works, which might, for example, decide to automate production, laying off thousands of workers. Or one's future may depend upon what a fashion magazine decides is 'this year's thing', placing those who sewed last year's thing out of work. But this objection, it appears, presupposes that people do have a right to a say in decisions that affect them, and, certainly as a general principle, this seems false. Nozick points to the 'Symphony of the Air' which could exist only in a financially worthwhile way for as long as Toscanini remained conductor. Toscanini's retirement would detrimentally affect all the members of the orchestra, but it would be difficult to make the case that his retirement should be conditional on their agreement. Of course, it might be argued that one such counter-example shows very little, but even conceiving of a scheme which really did grant people a worthwhile say over all important matters which affect them poses great difficulties. In matters affecting more than a few people the effect of one's vote would be so diluted as to be practically worthless.

Here it might be said that Nozick's reply misses the point of the criticism. The thought is not that the capitalist market economy should give people the right to a say in matters which affect them, for given the 'anarchic' structure of capitalist production, this would be impossible. Rather, a new type of economic organization of society is required, under which activity would be democratically planned and under the control of those it concerns. Thus it would naturally give people a say in matters which affect them. This, of course, has for a long time been an attractive idea, but we are still waiting to be shown how such a scheme could work in a desirable way. And even if it could work, we would still have to determine what its costs would be.

The second important strand of Marxist criticism of the capitalist market is that its existence depends upon the exploitation of the workers by capitalists. Indeed, it is often noted that Marx's theory of exploitation has two roles to play within Marxist theory: to explain how it is possible for capitalists to make a profit, and to demonstrate that capitalism is unjust. Marx explicitly declared that the theory of exploitation was required for the first, explanatory task, but whether he also intended to argue that capitalism is unjust has been a matter of controversy.[21] However, let us take it, for present purposes, that a critique of capitalism can be constructed on the basis of Marx's theory of exploitation, whether or not Marx himself had that project in mind.

The general idea behind a moral theory of exploitation is that to be exploited is to be used unfairly, or wrongly, used simply as a tool or instrument to another's purposes. Exploitation, thus, appears to be a form of injustice, but, perhaps more importantly, it appears to be failure to respect another as a person. Nozick, as we have seen, agrees with Kant that people should not be used simply as means to other's ends. But the charge under consideration is that libertarianism, via the market, will lead exactly to this.

Making out a charge of exploitation will depend, first, on arriving at a clear characterization of exploitation, second, on showing that exploitation in the sense characterized is wrong, and third, showing that under the circumstances in question, exploitation takes place. It is now often argued that Marx failed at the first hurdle. As part of his economic analysis, the theory of exploitation is embedded within Marx's now largely discredited labour theory of value, to which Nozick adds more acute objections. It is beyond the scope of the present work to examine Marx's labour theory of value and its problems,[22] but Marx's own definition of exploitation, which relies upon concepts from the labour theory of value, must be abandoned. This, however, is of little moment, for there is a way of reconstructing the Marxist theory of exploitation without relying on the labour theory of value. John Roemer has suggested that 'Marxian exploitation is defined as the unequal exchange of labour for goods: the exchange is unequal when the amount of labour embodied in the goods the worker can purchase with his income (which usually consists only of wage income) is less than the amount of labour he expended to earn that income.'[23] So if I work ten hours to earn £25, and with £25 I can only buy goods which took other people five hours to make, there has been an unequal exchange of labour for goods, and I am exploited. Thus on this account it is almost certain there will be exploitation under capitalism, for if a capitalist is to make a profit, then the worker must, each day, be paid less than the day's work has produced.

This account of exploitation seems to capture Marx's essential point, and so it should be no surprise that one objection made by Nozick to Marx's original theory also applies to this variant: according to this definition there will be exploitation in any society in which either there is investment for future growth, or those unable to work are subsidized by the labour of others. Thus there is no reason to think that exploitation is specific to capitalism, nor, indeed, that, for a Marxist, exploitation is always wrong. At the very least, this definition of exploitation requires modification and must make clear that the important point is not only that workers lose something when they are exploited, but that they lose it to someone who has no fair claim to it: the capitalist. The capitalist requires the worker to work on unfair terms.

But if terms of employment are unfair, why should the worker agree to them? The classic reply is that the worker has no option. Given no independent access to the means of production, and hence to the means of subsistence, it seems that the worker is forced to work for whatever terms the capitalist is offering, or starve. Thus there are two elements to the charge of exploitation: force and unfairness. Nozick's primary defence of capitalism is to try to show that workers are not forced to work for capitalists. If the workers are not forced to work for the capitalist, then, *a fortiori*, they are not forced to work on unfair terms, and thus they are not exploited.

So are workers forced to work for capitalists? On Nozick's own definition of forcing, we have seen, the answer is that they are not forced provided everyone acts within their rights. However, for the purposes of this discussion, Nozick initially appears prepared to accept a wider definition of force, in which you are forced to do X if you have no reasonable alternative to doing X. So, Nozick argues, no one is forced to work for a capitalist if there is a reasonable alternative. If, for example, there exists a public sector in which anyone who wishes to can work, this would count as a reasonable alternative. Thus, given the existence of such a sector, even if very few people decide to work in it, those who do choose to work for capitalists are not exploited. But then suppose no one decides to work in the public sector, for whatever reason, and so it withers away. Now there is no reasonable alternative to working for a capitalist, but it seems very strange to say that people are forced to work for a capitalist for this is what they have chosen to do, and would continue to choose to do even if they did have certain reasonable alternatives. Nozick's conclusion seems to be that in a free market, capitalism will not be exploitative because workers are not forced to work for capitalists in any important sense of force.

But this reply is unlikely to satisfy the critic of capitalism. Does exploitation really depend on the idea that workers are actually forced to work for capitalists? Another way of presenting the theory would be to say that you are exploited if the best option you have is to work on unfair terms (and the employer uses his knowledge of this to offer employment on such terms). Thus although exploitation relies upon a notion akin to forcing it is not the concept of force utilized by Nozick. On the classic idea of 'exploiting another's vulnerability' someone can be vulnerable even if they have various alternatives open to them, if all those alternatives are unattractive. If the capitalist takes advantage of this vulnerability to offer an unfair bargain, then the capitalist is an exploiter.

The best defence for the capitalist against the charge of exploitation seems, then, to be to argue that the terms of employment offered are not unfair. Nozick hints at a line of argument to defend the capitalist in this way. As was noted before, workers do have certain apparently preferable alternatives to working for capitalists. They might start up workers' co-operatives, or attempt to start their own businesses. Yet those workers who remain working for capitalists do not take these routes out. Why not? Nozick suggests that workers may prefer a steady wage than to run the risk of a loss-making business. Thus the possibility of large profits is traded for the security against large loss, to the fair mutual advantage of capitalist and worker. The terms of the contract, therefore, it could be argued, are not exploitative, but are a fair accommodation between two parties with different skills and different views about acceptable risks.

It may well be that some proportion of the present working class do make exactly the calculation Nozick supposes, and choose a relatively low-income, but ulcer-free, life, rather than engaging in risky, high stress, self-employment. But what proportion of workers have the opportunity to think in these terms? Particularly among the lower paid, the idea of starting up a business of their own may seem absurd. Could they really raise the capital? Would failure mean destitution? Can they even make a rational assessment of the risks? Might others collude to drive newcomers out of business? Thus a large percentage of the working population may view themselves as having no better option than to work on terms they consider unfair, that is to be exploited. But that these terms are in fact unfair, and that the workers have no better option than to work on such terms, is something that needs to be shown in detail, and it cannot simply be assumed that capitalism is necessarily a system of exploitation, according to any morally important concept of exploitation. But neither can it be assumed that capitalism does not involve exploitation.

The reactions of radicals to Nozick's criticisms will be mixed. Few, probably, will give up all their objections in the face of Nozick's replies. Many will simply refuse to listen. But those who have been prepared to do so have had to think very hard to find replies. One virtue of Nozick's work is that a great deal of honing and sharpening has had to be done to improve the rigour of radical objections to capitalism, once Nozick's defences are taken into account. It is no longer acceptable to criticize capitalism by platitude.

Libertarianism and Utopianism

To summarize the position so far, Nozick's arguments against the anarchist and the defender of the extensive state have not established the truth of libertarianism, but nevertheless Nozick has registered strong and important criticism of some of his most powerful rivals. Thus libertarianism is not proved, but in this respect it is probably no worse off than any other political philosophy at the present time. However, we have not yet explored all Nozick's strategies for defending the minimal state, for there remains a third: the idea of the minimal state as a 'framework for utopia'.

Throughout the critical literature, libertarianism has been identified with an extreme form of *laissez-faire* capitalism. At the centre stands property rights and the market. People's choices are unconstrained by any central, supervising authority. You are free to sell what you own (including yourself), and to buy whatever you can afford, at a price agreed with the vendor. But in response to this interpretation, it is important to make clear the distinction between what libertarianism permits, and what it recommends. Although libertarianism is obviously intended to permit unrestrained capitalism, it does not recommend it, for it recommends nothing. People are free to make whatever arrangements they wish. Thus, '[i]n this *laissez-faire* system it could turn out that though they are permitted, there are no actually functioning 'capitalist' institutions' (321). In fact, there are important aspects of contemporary capitalism which would actually appear inconsistent with libertarianism. Nozick discusses the question of whether the minimal state could allow limited liability. But what about corporate personality? And provision and regulation of the money supply? Each of these seem essential to capitalism as we now know it, but it is far from clear that they are all consistent with libertarian principles.[24]

Be this as it may, however, the main point is that libertarianism does not require capitalism. Libertarianism is concerned, essentially, with what people may claim from each other as of right, and this comes to non-interference with self and with property. But superimposed upon this structure of rights, Nozick envisages that 'communities' may flourish, in the form of voluntary organizations. In these one's commitments may go further than those one has within the minimal state. Communities may enforce regulations that the state may not. Remaining within the community may be conditional upon obeying those regulations; perhaps recognizing enforceable, positive obligations to others, or obeying rules governing religious, sexual, or intellectual practice.

Within the minimal state, then, there is room for utopia; not a single vision but a pluralist utopia. Whatever your idea of utopia, provided you can find enough others to populate and pay for it, then under libertarianism it is possible. The image conjured up is one in which anyone may go off with kindred spirits to live as they wish, far apart from others with whom they need have no dealings. One group may set up a community where they play wild music late into the night, and another may go off to spend their time in total silence, illuminating manuscripts, and distilling herbal liqueurs. Bored or disillusioned with what they have, people may leave their community and apply to join others. Some communities will wither, and others flourish.

How plausible is this picture? In the abstract it sounds very attractive. Why argue about whether society should be organized on capitalist or communist lines if the capitalists can go away and do what they want, while the communists can do what they want too.[25] But could this multiplicity really work? As Peter Singer writes: 'could a community that wanted a lot of redistribution survive the departure of the wealthy members whose moral principles are weaker than their desire for wealth? Could it withstand the pressure of applications to join from the down-and-outs left to starve in neighbouring communities run by ruthless capitalists?'[26]

A second criticism is that Nozick's image of people freely moving from one utopia to another until they find their heaven, ignores the thought that certain choices may be irreversible. If the members of our little self-sufficient rural communist community decide to sell up to try their hands as corporate raiders they may find that when they decide to return to their former style of life, land prices – owing, say, to the explosion of the 'Golf Village' style of utopia – are beyond their reach. This thought may lead to speculation about whether a law of evolution would apply to the plural utopias. Perhaps, in the long run, we may find the framework regulated by the law of the survival of the economically most fit and so we would expect to see a development not of diversity but of homogeniety. Those communities with great market power would eventually soak up all but the most resistant of those communities around them.

Nozick realizes that there are problems with the idea of the framework. Children present one such. At what age, for example, should they be able to leave? Do they have a right to be informed in a balanced way about alternative ways of life? If a society shares the belief that to discuss the theory of evolution is a sin, may they indoctrinate this belief in their children? If so, how can their children make free choices? If not, how is this to be regulated?

Finally, an important source of difficulty with the picture of a framework for utopia is whether there is space enough on this crowded earth for everyone to be able to do what they want without disturbing others, or at least without infringing upon their property rights. Although Nozick does recognize that overcrowding will lead to problems of relations between communities, his model appears appropriate only if there is plenty of space, and not many people. Nozick asks whether there would be large cities. But of course there would be, even if no one wants them, unless the birth-rate drops dramatically. As things are, Nozick's framework appears to be no more realistic than any other utopian vision.

Libertarianism, Liberalism, Conservatism

Recognition of libertarianism as a framework for utopia gives a clear indication of Nozick's pluralism, and that within his political vision there is great scope for people to live according to diverse, and even opposed, conceptions of the good. This observation suggests that Nozick's view is, essentially, a liberal one, being strongly neutral between different ways of life. Yet it seems much more commonly thought that Nozick should be labelled a conservative. The reason for this is not hard to find. A simplistic taxonomy of political views might lead one to argue that views have to be placed somewhere on the political spectrum, and, clearly, as Nozick is closer to the right than to the left, it follows that he is a conservative.

Nozick, however, never claims to be a conservative, and others with similar views refuse the label. Hayek's *Constitution of Liberty*, for example, contains a postscript entitled 'Why I am not a Conservative'. Furthermore, the theoretical conservative mainstream has hardly welcomed Nozick to its ranks. Roger Scruton, in his defence of conservatism, *The Meaning of Conservatism*, writes that the conservative emphasis on authority, constitution, institutions, tradition, custom, and allegiance are wholly incompatible with libertarian 'minimal statism'.[27] Moreover, concerning Nozick's view that 'taxation is nothing but forced labour and therefore inherently unjust', Scruton writes, 'if we are to concede such an argument then we abolish the conservative enterprise, and cease to acknowledge the web of obligations by which citizens are bound to each other and the state.'[28] Many traditional conservative beliefs – organicism, natural hierarchy, nationalism, divine intent in the design of society[29] – would simply be an embarrassment to Nozick.

It has often been thought that Nozick, in his emphasis upon *laissez-faire*, is closer in spirit to nineteenth-century Liberalism than to any other major political movement. However, in practical political terms there are too many theories to match each against a single political party, and it must be said that current parties of the right have increasingly added modern libertarian, *laissez-faire* doctrine to their traditional conservatism. Hence we see an uneasy, potentially unstable, mix of 'Old Right' and 'New Right' views coming to dominate what is still called conservative thinking.

The central connection between New and Old Right seems to be trenchant opposition to socialism and equality on the grounds of the defence of private property. Yet even here there is division over what type of property rights are worthy of defence. Within traditional conservative thinking there remains a vestige of the feudal idea of property, in which the possessor is not so much the individual but the family line, and in which the current owner acts partly as trustee, with responsibilities not just to descendants but also to the less fortunate. The idea of *noblesse oblige* still remains part of traditional conservatism. This recognition of non-voluntary obligations contrasts with libertarian property rights, which are centred on the owner's right to choose, and the only constraint on the use of property is that it must not be used in such a way as to violate the rights of others.[30] This difference will inevitably be reflected in policy judgements. Consider the question of whether a landed family should be permitted to demolish their country mansion, of great architectural and historical interest, and sell the site to an industrialist who intends to build a safe, but ugly, chemical plant. Modern conservatives should be pulled in both directions.

So although traditional conservatives and libertarians may form a political alliance, it is clear that important theoretical matters divide them. Indeed it is also worth sharply distinguishing two strands within libertarian or *laissez-faire* thought. The first is Nozick's rights-based stance: if we are to respect people's rights then we must have libertarianism, irrespective of its further consequences. The second is to argue that the *laissez-faire* free market is defensible on utilitarian grounds of economic efficiency. This approach is represented particularly in the works of Friedman, although in his work, and that of Hayek, both types of defence are present.

Nozick's libertarian position is based on rights, rather than economic efficiency; it allows him to countenance that people might use the market to contract out of it, perhaps into some extremely inefficient co-operative community. For as long as such a defection from the market is voluntary on the part of all concerned, then Nozick has no objection to it. For this reason, with the framework for utopia in mind, it seems better to think of libertarianism as a form of liberalism – hyper-liberalism – whose message is that what consenting adults get up to in their own time and (perhaps more importantly) their own space is entirely their own business. Certainly this is a breed of liberalism very far from the welfare liberalism, or liberal equality, of Rawls, but its emphasis on the idea of self-ownership, which has been seen by some as a key element of liberalism, and its toleration for diverse conceptions of the good, places libertarianism squarely within liberal theory.

But does libertarianism really display tolerance for diverse conceptions of the good? One reason for thinking that it may not is that, as we saw in Chapter 2, the foundation for libertarian rights is a view of 'the meaning of life'. In Nozick's view the important elements in a meaningful life are based on autonomy, rationality, and individual self-development, and so he fashioned a theory of rights to make available the type of life which furthers these goals. But as we saw, alternative theories of rights can also be claimed to correspond to this theory of the meaningful life, and other views of the meaningful life may give rise to yet more theories of rights. The point here is that the theory of the meaningful life will issue in a doctrine of rights most friendly to those conceptions of the good which bear the closest resemblance to that theory of the meaning-ful life.[31] Thus, for example, on Nozick's theory it may turn out that it is very easy to live a life of independent self-reliance, but much more difficult to put oneself into a network of mutual, 'non-voluntary' obligations in which one has claims to the aid of others, and recognizes that they have claims to aid too. Or to use another example, the sunset lover has far greater assurance that his or her pleasures will be obtainable than the movie lover, for that depends on others being motivated to make movies.

It could be argued, however, that this is as it should be. The consequence of Nozick's view is that the more people one's conception of the good depends upon, other things being equal, then the more difficult it would be to lead that life. Although libertarian society makes certain conceptions of the good easier to live than others, it is hard to see how any society could be absolutely neutral. Encouraging and discouraging on the grounds of the numbers involved seems a fair way of dealing with unavoid-able bias. The important thing is to make sure no type of life is absolutely ruled out, unless it violates the rights of others, and, in theory, this is what libertarianism achieves. What would actually develop in a libertarian society is quite another matter, and we saw in the last section that we may not have much reason to be optimistic about this.

The Lure of Libertarianism

Finally, what are the achievements of *Anarchy, State, and Utopia*? Nozick has very few disciples in academic political philosophy, yet almost every book published on justice, property, or political obligation in the last decade and a half contains discussions of, or at least references to, his work. With Rawls, Nozick continues to dominate political philosophy. But why should this be so, if so few philosophers agree with what he has to say?

The first virtue of *Anarchy, State, and Utopia* is that it forcefully presents a position in political philosophy which is striking, powerful, uncompromising, and original at least in so far as such a view had not been presented to the mainstream of academic philosophy for a century, and never with such vigour. But it is not simply the views presented which have made such an impact, but the manner in which they are presented. The book bristles with arguments of great ingenuity, alarming and bizarre counter-examples to comfortable views, presented with wit, and some-times, corn. Political philosophy had not been done like this before, and has rarely been so abstract and so clever. Also it is rare that a single work has managed to challenge so many received views. Finally, *Anarchy, State, and Utopia* attracts attention because it represents an extreme position. Thus it marks out one of the boundaries of political philosophy and so receives attention from all those who wish to stop short.

Nozick's extremism is a consequence of taking one concept and applying it without restraint to all areas of political philosophy. It would be a natural assumption that the concept lying behind libertarianism is liberty. Though natural, this is mistaken. We saw in Chapter 4 that Nozick's conception of liberty is particularly etiolated, and formal. Your liberty is your right to act within the moral law – a right to do what you have a right to do. Hence, more fundamental is the catalogue of those rights, and that catalogue is based on the idea of ownership. Thus Nozick's political philosophy consists in taking the idea that one has absolute rights of private ownership of oneself, and of those bits of the world one rightfully possesses, as far as it possibly can be taken. This is why the rhetoric of ownership plays such a large part in *Anarchy, State, and Utopia*; various welfare provisions, for example, are criticized on the grounds that they make others your 'part owner'.

It is remarkable (and, indeed, often remarked) that, although the entire edifice of libertarianism rests on these ideas of absolute property rights over self and world, they themselves are given so little by way of defence. But, on the other hand, Nozick's emphasis on historical considerations of ownership has come as a salutary reminder to utilitarians, egalitarians, and welfare economists that political philosophy cannot restrict itself to ideas of need or efficiency. We must not overlook that people own things and believe that they have very strong moral title over what they own. Entitlement theory strikes an intuitive chord with many people, and is an important aspect of our moral and political life. Nozick's main achievement is to bring the concept of rights firmly back into the middle of debate in political philosophy.

But although entitlement is important, is it of sole importance? Considerations of need, desert, and efficiency also strike an intuitive chord. Bernard Williams suggests that Nozick's conception of justice looks like 'an enormous exaggeration of at best one aspect of our moral ideas'.[32] Political philosophy consists, in part, of taking all those values relevant to the political sphere, examining their relations and investigating how much of what we value we can have. Do we need to compromise some or all of our values, or, properly understood, do they cohere? One way of understanding libertarianism is that it finesses the trading and trimming of values, by focusing on one – ownership – and pushing it to the limit, at the expense, if necessary, of all else. We learn a great deal in seeing how far this can be taken.

The lure of libertarianism is that it cuts through the confusing tangle of diverging values, presenting a simple, clear, and principled approach to political philosophy – a decision procedure for politics, which instructs us that we will be doing all that is required of us if we respect others' rights of self-ownership and thing-ownership. Our two fundamental questions must be whether this picture is coherent – can things be this simple? – and whether it is convincing – do we want things like this?

We have, I think, seen the great strain libertarianism comes under in the attempt to make it consistent. First, Nozick has to introduce increasingly *ad hoc* and implausible principles to justify the minimal state, and even then the attempt at justification, although ingenious, fails. Second, initial private appropriation remains undefended by Nozick, and this may well be because it is indefensible on libertarian grounds. Allowing people virtually unlimited appropriation of the world will importantly restrict what others can do, thus undermining their liberty and self-ownership. Thus Nozick's concept of ownership itself generates conflicts, and so the project of allowing no restrictions upon ownership itself falls into incoherence.

Even setting aside the inconsistencies, how attractive is libertarianism? I think we must agree with Williams – it is at best part of what we want. We cannot ignore need, desert, and other values. But does this mean that entitlement is just one more value fighting for priority? This is certainly one way of looking at matters. However, entitlement considerations do have great, intuitive, day-to-day appeal. The fact, for example, that it is my money seems to silence claims that you need it, deserve it, or that the world would be a happier place if you had it. To do justice to this we might adopt a suggestion from Rawls and distinguish the basic structure of justice from the legitimate expectations that arise within that structure.[33] In setting up a system of basic justice, we may incorporate many diverse values. There may be, for example, many different reasons why we make people pay taxes. But having set up the structure, by law, it is important that people are able to rely on, by and large, its continuity. It would be wrong, for example, greatly to adjust the rate of taxation from month to month, for people would have extreme difficulty planning their lives rationally. Thus, within any structure of basic justice, people come to form legitimate expectations – their entitlements – and these will loom larger in their lives than the values in pursuit of which the structure is set up.

From this Rawlsian point of view, the error of libertarianism is to take principles of legitimate expectations from within the structure and claim that the structure should be formed in accordance with those principles. That is, all claims of entitlement, are for Rawls, relative to a prior structure of justice. Nothing is 'mine absolutely' but only 'mine given the rules'. Libertarianism forgets this essential relativism of claims of entitlement. Thus we can accept the great appeal of entitlement principles, yet also argue that they do not constitute the deepest truth about justice.

Of course, this reply is only a suggestion, and I have done

nothing to argue for it. Nozick would deny that he has made any such mistake, and whatever our view of this we should credit Nozick with something of the greatest importance. He has opened a new option – defined a new place on the spectrum of views – in serious political philosophy. This has been to the great enrichment of political philosophy, invigorating debate and helping to generate a level of activity in the subject unseen for decades. In pursuing his one-valued political philosophy Nozick has pushed the concept of ownership further than perhaps ever before, exploring issues which, in a more balanced and compromising view, might have remained unexplored. Given the eclectic nature of his academic writings, to call Nozick narrow in vision could scarcely be more inappropriate. Nevertheless, in so far as his political philosophy is concerned, Mill's phrase 'a one-eyed man', seems particularly apposite for Nozick. It is often by the obsessions of the one-eyed that philosophy advances, and we should end by concurring with Mill's judgement that:

> For our own part, we have a large tolerance for one-eyed men, provided their one eye is a penetrating one: if they saw more, they probably would not see so keenly, nor so eagerly pursue one course of inquiry.[34]

Notes

Introduction

1 J. Rawls, *A Theory of Justice* (Oxford University Press, Oxford, 1972), p. viii.
2 A point made by R. P. Wolff, 'Robert Nozick's Derivation of the Minimal State', in *Reading Nozick*, ed. J. Paul (Blackwell, Oxford, 1982), p. 82.
3 See J. S. Mill, *Utilitarianism*, ed. Mary Warnock (Collins, Glasgow, 1962); J. Bentham, *An Introduction to the Principles of Morals and Legislation* (Methuen, London, 1982); H. Sidgwick, *Methods of Ethics* (Macmillan, London, 1907).
4 See I. Berlin, 'Two Concepts of Liberty', in his *Four Essays on Liberty* (Oxford University Press, Oxford, 1969), pp. 118–72; B. Williams, 'Conflicts of Values', in his *Moral Luck* (Cambridge University Press, Cambridge, 1981), pp. 71–82; C. Taylor, 'The Diversity of Goods', in his *Philosophy and the Human Sciences* (Cambridge University Press, Cambridge, 1985), pp. 230–47; T. Nagel 'The Fragmentation of Value', in his *Mortal Questions* (Cambridge University Press, Cambridge, 1979), pp. 128–41.
5 R. Tuck, *Natural Rights Theories: Their Origin and Development* (Cambridge University Press, Cambridge, 1979), p. 1.

Chapter 1 *Nozick's Libertarianism*

1 B. Tucker, *State Socialism and Anarchy*, in *The Anarchist Reader*, ed. G. Woodcock (Fontana, Glasgow, 1977), p. 151.
2 This criticism was originally made by J. Rawls, *A Theory of Justice*

(Oxford University Press, Oxford, 1972), pp. 22–7.

3 The analogy of 'forcible redistribution of bodily parts' comes from Nozick, p. 206. The example of the eye lottery is from G. A. Cohen, 'Self-Ownership, World-Ownership, and Equality', in *Justice and Equality Here and Now*, ed. F. S. Lucash (Cornell University Press, Ithaca, NY, 1986), p. 111. See also John Harris, 'The Survival Lottery', *Philosophy*, 50 (1977), pp. 81–7.

4 This image is from F. Hayek, *The Constitution of Liberty* (Routledge & Kegan Paul, London, 1960), p. 139.

5 See, for example, David Lloyd Thomas, *In Defence of Liberalism* (Blackwell, Oxford, 1988), ch. 1.

6 In essence, I owe this phrase to H. L. A. Hart, 'Between Utility and Rights', in *The Idea of Freedom*, ed. A. Ryan (Oxford University Press, 1979), p. 81. However, as we shall see in the next chapter, Hart is not quite right to say that, for Nozick, rights fill the whole *moral* landscape.

7 M. Friedman and R. Friedman, *Free To Choose* (Penguin, Harmondsworth, Middlesex, 1980), pp. 57–8.

8 For an illuminating survey, see F. E. Manuel and F. P. Manuel, *Utopian Thought in the Western World* (Blackwell, Oxford, 1979).

Chapter 2   *Libertarian Rights*

1 See David Miller, *Anarchism* (Dent, London, 1984), for a good survey.

2 H. Sidgwick, *Methods of Ethics* (Macmillan, London, 1907), p. 382.

3 See, for example, Sidgwick, *Methods of Ethics*, or R. M. Hare, *Moral Thinking* (Oxford University Press, Oxford, 1981).

4 For this point, see T. Nagel, 'Equality', in his *Mortal Questions* (Cambridge University Press, Cambridge, 1979), pp. 106–27.

5 'Whatever the consequences' perhaps needs qualification. Might the consequences ever be so severe that a violation of rights becomes justified? Nozick seems unsure. 'The question of whether these side-constraints are absolute, or whether they may be violated in order to avoid catastrophic moral horror . . . is one I hope largely to avoid' (30). For a discussion of how Nozick's view could be amended to allow, among other things, for the interference with rights to avoid moral horror, see J. J. Thomson, 'Some Ruminations on Rights', in *Reading Nozick*, ed. J. Paul (Blackwell, Oxford, 1982), pp. 130–47.

6 This example is adapted from an idea of Simon Evnine.

7 R. Nozick, *Philosophical Explanations* (Oxford University Press, Oxford, 1981), p. 502.

8 More subtle cases in which there may be a clash of rights even on Nozick's theory will be investigated in Chapter 3.

9   H. L. A. Hart, 'Are There Any Natural Rights?', in *Theories of Rights*, ed. J. Waldron (Oxford University Press, Oxford, 1984), pp. 77–8.

10 J. Bentham, *Anarchical Fallacies*, in *Nonsense upon Stilts*, ed. Jeremy Waldron (Methuen, London, 1987), p. 73.

11 Bentham, *ibid.*, p. 53.

12 R. Dworkin, *Taking Rights Seriously* (Duckworth, London, 1977), p. 177.

13 J. Locke, *Second Treatise*, in his *Two Treatises On Civil Government* (Cambridge University Press, Cambridge, 1960), s. 4.

14 Locke, *ibid.*, s. 4.

15 Locke, *ibid.*, s. 6.

16 Locke, *First Treatise*, s. 42. However, it is not clear that Locke intended such rights to be legally enforceable.

17 I. Kant, *Groundwork of the Metaphysic of Morals*, in H. J. Paton, *The Moral Law* (Hutchinson, London, 1948), p. 91.

18 I owe this point to Michael Rosen.

19 Although of course Hobbes would not agree that we have natural rights.

20 T. Hobbes, *Leviathan*, ed. C. B. Macpherson (Penguin, Harmondsworth, Middlesex, 1968), p. 186.

21 See especially her novel, *The Fountainhead* (New American Library, New York, 1952).

22 For Nozick's most detailed criticism of Rand, although not including this point, see 'On the Randian Argument', in *Reading Nozick*, pp. 206–31.

23 S. Scheffler, 'Natural Rights, Equality, and the Minimal State', in *Reading Nozick*, p. 153.

24 Scheffler, *ibid.*, p. 153.

25 Locke, *Second Treatise*, s. 16.

26 Locke, *ibid.*, s. 8.

Chapter 3   *Defending the Minimal State*

1   Unless, implausibly, the shortfall could be made up by voluntary subscriptions or other commercial activities.

2   J. Locke, *Second Treatise*, in his *Two Treatises On Civil Government* (Cambridge University Press, Cambridge, 1960), s. 14.

3   B. Russell, *Political Ideals* (George Allen & Unwin, London, 1963), pp. 19–20.

4   Locke, *Second Treatise*, s. 13.

5   Locke, *ibid.*, s. 119.

6   D. Hume, 'Of the Original Contract', in his *Essays Moral Political and Literary*, ed. E. F. Miller (Liberty Press, Indianapolis, Ind., 1985), p. 475.

7   By Murray N. Rothbard, *The Ethics of Liberty* (Humanities Press, Atlantic Highlands, NJ, 1982), p. 229.

8   Given the existence of property it is plausible that exchange and money would also exist in the state of nature.

9   What about force by independents against other independents? I return to this below.

10 Rothbard, *The Ethics of Liberty*, p. 247.

11 Not all commentators agree. Robert Paul Wolff, for example, argues that the purpose of Nozick's argument is 'to establish the *possibility* of a *de jure* legitimate state' ('Robert Nozick's Derivation of the Minimal State', in *Reading Nozick*, ed. J. Paul, (Blackwell, Oxford, 1982), p. 80).

12 Nozick, too, has been read as intending such an argument. Bernard Williams writes: 'it is Mr Nozick's thought, certainly in his theory of justice, and I take it here, that how a state of affairs actually arose is crucial for its acceptability' ('The Minimal State', in *Reading Nozick*, p. 33.) As the argument of this section implies, I think Williams is mistaken here.

13 C. G. Hempel, *Aspects of Scientific Explanation* (Free Press, New York, 1965), p. 246.

14 See Robert Holmes, 'Nozick on Anarchism', in *Reading Nozick*, p. 59.

15 Nozick distinguishes between political philosophy and explanatory political theory, which we might also call political science. Nozick introduces the idea of 'potential explanations' not to defend the state (justify it) but to explain why it has certain features. Thus, for example, we might want an explanation of why the state, in fact, claims a monopoly of force. But this is a different question from the (normative) issue of whether the state is justified if it makes this claim.

16 For a fuller discussion of the problem of political obligation, see J. Wolff, 'What is the Problem of Political Obligation?', *Proceedings of the Aristotelian Society*, 91 (1990–1), forthcoming.

17 For an examination and critique of assumptions of this nature see Amartya Sen, 'Rational Fools', in *Philosophy and Economic Theory*, ed. F. Hahn and M. Hollis (Oxford University Press, Oxford, 1977), pp. 87–109.

18 There may be problems about avenging the dead, unless we also assume that rights to punish can be inherited in the same way that private property rights might be.

19 This point is raised by J. E. J. Altham, 'Reflections on the State of Nature', in *Rational Action*, ed. R. Harrison (Cambridge University Press, Cambridge, 1980), pp. 136–7.

20 Another possible reply is that the division-of-labour gain from the

employment of the protection agency will allow clients to cover its expenses. Now I do not have to spend time protecting myself, I can produce more wheat. I owe this point to G. A. Cohen.

21 B. Williams, 'The Minimal State', in *Reading Nozick*, p. 33.

22 Locke, *Second Treatise*, s. 93.

23 This problem is related to many others of similar structure in rational choice theory, often referred to as the 'Prisoner's Dilemma'. For a good collection of articles on such themes see *Rational Man and Irrational Society*, ed. B. Barry and R. Hardin (Sage, Beverly Hills, Calif., 1982). See also F. Hirsch, *Social Limits to Growth* (Harvard University Press, Cambridge, Mass., 1976), p. 40, for the concept of 'the tyranny of small decision making'.

24 I owe this observation to Willie Watts Miller.

25 For this reason violation of rights to life, person, and liberty will generally be prohibited and punished, even if compensation is offered.

26 It is not wholly clear that 'great benefit' is considered a condition by Nozick: his point might just be that if the violation does not create such benefits then compensation would be uneconomic, and so no one would have a reason for engaging in such a violation.

27 J. Paul, 'The Withering of Nozick's Minimal State', in *Reading Nozick*, p. 72.

28 One reason is that he thinks that this version of the principle is weaker than a version which reads: 'If someone knows that doing act A would violate Q's rights unless condition C obtained, he may not do A if he does not know that C obtains' (106). If we read 'ascertain' in the final version as the dictionary instructs us to, then, in fact, the final version is no weaker than this principle requiring us not only to know whether C obtains, but to have used the best feasible means of coming to know this.

29 It is worth noting that to decide whether or not the epileptic – or anyone – has a right to drive, one needs to be much clearer than Nozick is, or perhaps can be, about when precisely people have a right to inflict risks on others.

Chapter 4 *The Entitlement Theory of Justice*

1 For a particularly striking and original presentation of such statistics see J. Pen, *Income Distribution* (Penguin, Harmondsworth, Middlesex, 1971), pp. 48–59.

2 J. Rawls, *A Theory of Justice* (Oxford University Press, Oxford, 1972).

3 G. A. Cohen has argued that the term 'justice in holdings' is also non-neutral, for it suggests a picture of ownership *rights*. The term

'justice in access to goods' is, perhaps, more nearly neutral.

4 Matters here become confusing for despite saying that patterned theories are a subclass of historical theories Nozick also allows that the principle 'distribute according to I.Q.' is patterned, but not historical (156). It may often be hard to decide whether to count a theory as 'end-state' or 'patterned'. However, this is of little consequence as the important distinction is between those theories which are 'historical unpatterned' and those which are not.

5 For the case that a wide variety of theories may all have a claim to be called entitlement theories, in the sense of being historical and non-patterned, see R. van der Veen and P. Van Parijs, 'Entitlement Theories of Justice: From Nozick to Roemer and Beyond', *Economics and Philosophy*, 1 (1985), pp. 69–81.

6 D. Hume, *An Enquiry concerning the Principles of Morals*, in his *Enquiries*, 3rd edn., ed. Selby-Bigge (Oxford University Press, Oxford, 1975), section 3, part 2, p. 194.

7 A. Thiers, *De la propriété*, cited in R. Schlatter *Private Property, History of an Idea* (George Allen & Unwin, London, 1951), p. 236.

8 G. A. Cohen, 'Robert Nozick and Wilt Chamberlain: How Patterns Preserve Liberty', *Erkenntis*, 11 (1977), p. 15.

9 Cohen, *ibid.*, p. 15.

10 We will see a qualification to this statement of the principle later in this chapter.

11 See G. A. Cohen 'The Structure of Proletarian Unfreedom', in his *History, Labour, and Freedom* (Oxford University Press, Oxford, 1988), p. 256.

12 For further discussion of exploitation, see Chapter 5.

13 See Kirzner, 'Entrepreneurship, Entitlement, and Economic Justice', in *Reading Nozick*, ed. J. Paul (Blackwell, Oxford, 1982), pp. 383–411 for a discussion of the role of error in entrepreneurial activity.

14 E. Quest, 'Whatever Arises from a Just Distribution by Just Steps Is Itself Just', *Analysis*, 37 (1977), pp. 204–8.

15 Clearly this is a special case of the problem of collectively irrational consequences of individually rational action. See Chapter 3.

16 Cohen, 'Robert Nozick and Wilt Chamberlain', p. 12.

17 H. Steiner, 'Justice and Entitlement', in *Reading Nozick*, p. 382.

18 However to refute Nozick's principle of justice in transfer is not in itself to establish that patterned theories are correct. Some other procedural theory may hold the truth.

19 Nozick, of course, recognizes that not all taxation is taxation of labour, and suggests that the argument can be extended to include 'interest, entrepreneurial profits, and so on' (170).

20 Milton and Rose Friedman, *Free to Choose* (Penguin, Harmondsworth, Middlesex, 1980), p. 89.

21 Of course, it is open to Nozick's opponent to argue that some forms of forced labour are acceptable. Not all would disapprove of conscripting the voluntarily unemployed into community service. I owe this point to Anthony Skillen.

22 Cf H. L. A. Hart 'Between Utility and Rights', in *The Idea of Freedom*, ed. A. Ryan (Oxford University Press, Oxford, 1979), pp. 77–98.

23 J. Rawls, 'Social Unity and Primary Goods', in *Utilitarianism and Beyond*, ed. Amartya Sen and Bernard Williams (Cambridge University Press, Cambridge, 1982), p. 169.

24 C. Ryan, 'Yours, Mine and Ours: Property Rights and Individual Liberty', in *Reading Nozick*, pp. 323–43.

25 See, in particular, A. M. Honore, 'Ownership', in *Oxford Essays in Jurisprudence*, ed. A. G. Guest (Oxford University Press, London, 1961), pp. 107–47. Also L. C. Becker, *Property Rights* (Routledge & Kegan Paul, Boston, 1977) and J. Waldron, *The Right to Private Property* (Oxford University Press, Oxford, 1988).

26 T. Nagel, 'Libertarianism without Foundations', in *Reading Nozick*, p. 201.

27 I owe this formulation to Jonathan Wilwerding.

28 J. Bentham, *Anarchical Fallacies*, in *Nonsense upon Stilts*, ed. Jeremy Waldron (Methuen, London, 1987), p. 57.

29 See Cohen, *History Labour and Freedom*, pp. 239–304; and A. Gibbard, 'Natural Property Rights', *Nous*, 10 (1976), pp. 77–86.

30 See Charles Taylor 'What's Wrong with Negative Liberty', in his *Philosophy and the Human Sciences*, Philosophical Papers vol. 2 (Cambridge University Press, Cambridge, 1985), pp. 211–29; and O. O'Neill, 'The Most Extensive Liberty', *Proceedings of the Aristotelian Society*, 80 (1979/80), pp. 45–59.

31 M. Friedman, *Capitalism and Freedom* (Chicago University Press, Chicago, Ill., 1962), pp. 16–17.

32 C. B. Macpherson, 'Elegant Tombstones: A Note on Friedman's Freedoms', in his *Democratic Theory: Essays in Retrieval* (Oxford University Press, Oxford, 1973), p. 150.

33 J. J. Rousseau, *Discourse on Inequality* (Penguin, Harmondsworth, Middlesex, 1984), p. 109.

34 Quoted in Rousseau, *ibid.*, p. 180.

35 J. Locke, *Second Treatise*, in his *Two Treatises On Civil Government* (Cambridge University Press, Cambridge, 1960), s. 26.

36 J. J. Rousseau, *Social Contract* (Penguin, Harmondsworth, Middlesex, 1968), p. 67. For a partial reply see Becker, *Property Rights*, pp. 33–4.

37 See Karl Olivercrona, 'Locke's Theory of Appropriation', *Philosophical Quarterly*, 24 (1974), pp. 231–4.

38 For a detailed criticism of Locke's position, see also G. A. Cohen

'Marx and Locke on Land and Labour', *Proceedings of the British Academy*, 71 (1985), pp. 357–88.

39 See also, O. O'Neill, 'The Great Maxims of Justice and Charity', in her *Constructions of Reason* (Cambridge University Press, Cambridge, 1989), pp. 219–33.

40 O. O'Neill, 'Nozick's Entitlements', in *Reading Nozick*, p. 316.

41 For further reasons for this conclusion, see O'Neill, *ibid.*

42 H. Spencer, *Social Statics* (London, Chapman, 1851), p. 132. Spencer later changed his views on property. The chapter of *Social Statics* from which this quotation is taken ('The Right to the Use of the Land') was omitted from the later edition.

43 B. Tucker, *Instead of a Book* (B. R. Tucker, New York, 1893), p. 61.

44 I owe these points to Jonathan Dick.

45 Gibbard, 'Natural Property Rights'.

46 D. Lyons, 'The New Indian Claims and Original Rights to Land', in *Reading Nozick*, pp. 355–79.

47 See A. Kuflik, 'Process and End State in the Theory of Economic Justice', *Social Theory and Practice*, 8 (1982), pp. 73–94.

48 Lyons, 'The New Indian Claims', p. 362.

49 G. A. Cohen, 'Self-Ownership, World-Ownership, and Equality', in *Justice and Equality Here and Now*, ed. F. S. Lucash (Cornell University Press, Ithaca, NY, 1986), pp. 108–35.

50 Cohen, *ibid.*, p. 133.

51 For a further objection to Nozick's proposal for the setting of baselines, see G. S. Kavka, 'An Internal Critique of Nozick's Entitlement Theory', *Pacific Philosophical Quarterly*, 63 (1982), pp. 371–80.

52 Lyons, 'The New Indian Claims', pp. 355–79.

Chapter 5 *Nozick and Political Philosophy*

1 This is taken from J. Rawls, *A Theory of Justice* (Oxford University Press, Oxford, 1972), p. 302, with the reference to the 'just savings principle' omitted. Rawls has refined his account of these principles in subsequent formulations, but the differences are immaterial for present purposes.

2 For discussion of this argument see the papers collected in *Reading Rawls*, ed. N. Daniels (Blackwell, Oxford, 1975).

3 Rawls, *A Theory of Justice*, p. 4.

4 This may not strictly be true, as Nozick notes, for the worst off under one distribution might not be the worst off under another. However, this does not seem seriously to affect the point.

5 Rawls, *A Theory of Justice*, p. 312.

6 For a discussion of whether this is the correct way to read Rawls's reply see G. A. Cohen 'On The Currency of Egalitarian Justice', *Ethics*, 99 (1989), p. 914–15.

7 M. Sandel, *Liberalism and the Limits of Justice* (Cambridge University Press, Cambridge, 1982).

8 See J. Rawls 'Justice as Fairness: Political Not Metaphysical', *Philosophy and Public Affairs*, 14 (1985), pp. 223–51; A. Gutmann, 'Communitarian Critics of Liberalism', *Philosophy and Public Affairs*, 14 (1985), pp. 308–22.

9 Sandel, *Liberalism and the Limits of Justice*, pp. 89–92.

10 T. M. Scanlon, 'The Significance of Choice', in *The Tanner Lectures on Human Values*, vol. 7, ed. S. McMurry (University of Utah Press, Salt Lake City, 1988), pp. 186–88. Scanlon himself develops this point in a somewhat different context, and notes that it is not so much a way of answering Nozick, but a way of restating the disagreement between Rawls and Nozick.

11 B. Williams, 'The Idea of Equality', in his *Problems of the Self* (Cambridge University Press, Cambridge, 1973), p. 240.

12 For an attempt to improve upon Williams's argument by distinguishing needs and essential needs, see Paul Russell, 'Nozick, Need and Charity', *Journal of Applied Philosophy*, 4 (1987), pp. 205–16.

13 M. Walzer, *Spheres of Justice* (Blackwell, Oxford, 1983), p. 88n.

14 Joseph Heller, *Picture This* (Macmillan, London, 1988), p. 122.

15 Cf D. Sachs, 'How to Distinguish Self-Respect from Self-Esteem', *Philosophy and Public Affairs*, 10 (1981), pp. 346–60.

16 A. Skillen, *Ruling Illusions* (Harvester, Hassocks, Sussex, 1977) p. 49.

17 For a discussion of this suggestion see next section.

18 See also H. Braverman, *Labour and Monopoly Capital* (Monthly Review Press, New York, 1984).

19 See, for example, M. Walzer's discussion of the San Francisco Scavengers, in his *Spheres of Justice*, p. 177–8.

20 For a further, empirical, collection of woes of worker management economies among other things, see Alec Nove, *The Economics of Feasible Socialism* (George Allen & Unwin, London, 1983), esp. pp. 133–41. See also D. Miller, *Market, State, and Community* (Oxford University Press, Oxford, 1989).

21 See S. Lukes, *Marxism and Morality* (Oxford University Press, Oxford, 1987); and N. Geras, 'The Controversy about Marx and Justice', in *Marxist Theory*, ed. A. Callinicos (Oxford University Press, Oxford, 1989), pp. 211–67.

22 See P. Sweezy, *The Theory of Capitalist Development* (Monthly Review Press, New York, 1942) for a statement and defence of the

labour theory of value. J. Elster, *Making Sense of Marx* (Cambridge University Press, Cambridge, 1985), chap. 3, contains a good account of recent criticism.

23 J. Roemer, 'Should Marxists Be Interested in Exploitation?' in *Analytical Marxism*, ed. J. Roemer (Cambridge University Press, Cambridge, 1986), p. 260. For further interesting discussion of this topic, see the papers collected in *Modern Theories of Exploitation*, ed. A. Reeve (Sage, London, 1987).

24 I owe these points to Michael Rosen. See also F. Hayek, *The Constitution of Liberty* (Routledge & Kegan Paul, London, 1960), chap. 15, for an account of the respects in which an efficiently run capitalism presupposes that the state takes on a more-than-minimal function.

25 In 'Who Would Choose Socialism?', *Reason* (May 1978), pp. 22–3, Nozick argues that in Israel, where the existence of the Kibbutz gives people a real choice between Socialism and Capitalism, even on generous assumptions fewer than 9 per cent of the population have chosen to live under Socialism. There are, of course, other possible interpretations of these data. Perhaps fewer than 9 per cent choose to leave the mainstream, whatever it is.

26 Peter Singer, 'The Right to be Rich or Poor', in *Reading Nozick*, ed. J. Paul (Blackwell, Oxford, 1982), p. 38.

27 R. Scruton, *The Meaning of Conservatism* (Macmillan, London, 1984), p. 31.

28 Scruton, *ibid.*, p. 106.

29 See Russell Kirk, '*The Conservative Mind*' (Henry Regnery, Chicago, Ill., 1953).

30 For a discussion of how many different forms private property rights might take, see R. Schlatter, *Private Property, History of an Idea* (George Allen & Unwin, London, 1951).

31 The idea that one's political theory will in large part depend upon one's view of human nature or the nature of society has become commonplace. For one important study which emphasizes this point, see David Miller *Social Justice* (Oxford University Press, Oxford, 1976).

32 B. Williams, 'The Minimal State', in *Reading Nozick*, p. 34.

33 Rawls, *A Theory of Justice*, pp. 310–15. See also his 'The Basic Structure as Subject', *American Philosophical Quarterly*, 14 (1977), pp. 159–65.

34 J. S. Mill, 'Bentham', in *Utilitarianism*, ed. Mary Warnock (Collins, Glasgow, 1962), p. 98.

Guide to Further Reading

The starting point of contemporary Anglo-American political philosophy is J. Rawls, *A Theory of Justice* (especially parts 1 and 2). N. Daniels (ed.), *Reading Rawls,* is a very useful collection of critical articles. Further developments, clarifications, and refinements of Rawls's view can be found in his Dewey Lectures, 'Kantian Constructivism in Moral Theory', and in 'Justice as Fairness: Political not Metaphysical'. The main themes of *Anarchy, State, and Utopia* have received very unequal attention from Nozick's critics. Predictably, perhaps, Nozick's attempt to refute the anarchist has stimulated responses primarily from those sympathetic to anarchism; see M. N. Rothbard, *The Ethics of Liberty;* R. Holmes, 'Nozick on Anarchism'; and R. P. Wolff, 'The Derivation of the Minimal State'. Like many of the papers referred to in this book, those by Holmes and Wolff are reprinted in J. Paul (ed.), *Reading Nozick.* For background reading, D. Miller, *Anarchism,* is a good general guide to the topic, while G. Woodcock, *The Anarchist Reader,* is a very interesting selection from the major Anarchist thinkers. R. P. Wolff, *In Defence of Anarchism,* is an attempt to defend what has become known as 'philosophical anarchism'. For good, wider discussion see A. J. Simmons, *Moral Principles and Political Obligation.*

Nozick's idea that the minimal state is a framework for utopia has been the subject of very little discussion, although it is touched on by P. Singer, in 'The Right to be Rich or Poor'. For a detailed account of pre-Nozickian utopian theory, see F. E. Manuel and

F. P. Manuel, *Utopian Thought in the Western World.*

The position is quite different when we turn to the related topics of Nozick's theory of rights and his theory of justice. Here the response to Nozick – directly and indirectly – has been enormous. Key issues of discussion here are the consequences of libertarianism, and its relation to liberty; the structure and content of Nozick's theory of rights; self-ownership and private property; the free market; exploitation; equality; and the rehabilitation of distributive justice.

In a number of papers H. Steiner has urged the case that a basically libertarian theory of rights requires distributional equality. One lively expression of Steiner's view is 'Liberty and Equality', but also see his 'The Structure of a Set of Compossible Rights'; 'The Natural Right to the Means of Production'; 'Land, Liberty, and the early Herbert Spencer'; and, 'Individual Liberty'. A. Sen, in opposition to Nozick's idea of rights as side-constraints, has explored a system of 'goal-rights', i.e. a utilitarianism of rights; see 'Rights and Agency'. For related criticism see H. L. A. Hart, 'Between Utility and Rights'. Others have retained the form of Nozick's theory of rights, but rejected the anti-welfarist content; see S. Scheffler, 'Natural Rights, Equality, and the Minimal State', and H. Shue, *Basic Rights*. For background material on the topic of rights, J. Waldron (ed.), *Theories of Rights*, is a good collection of essays, while *Nonsense upon Stilts*, also edited by J. Waldron, contains attacks on the idea of natural rights by Bentham, Burke, and Marx.

The topic of private property rights has received a great deal of attention since the publication of *Anarchy, State, and Utopia*. Good introductory works, in which Nozick's theory is discussed, are A. Carter, *The Philosophical Foundation of Property Rights*; J. O. Grunebaum, *Private Ownership*; A. Reeve, *Property*; and A. Ryan, *Property*. More advanced is J. Waldron, *The Right to Private Property*.

The relation between self-ownership and ownership of things in the world has been explored by G. A. Cohen in two papers: 'Self-Ownership, World-Ownership, and Equality', and 'Self-Ownership, World-Ownership, and Equality: Part II'. Also, in a series of papers, Cohen has launched a powerful critical attack on the idea that libertarianism advances freedom. Some of these have now been reprinted in part 3 of his *History, Labour and Freedom*, but also see Cohen's 'Illusions about Private Property and Freedom'.

Recent discussion of liberty in political philosophy can be traced back to I. Berlin, 'Two Concepts of Liberty'. For criticism of Berlin, see C. Taylor, 'What's Wrong with Negative Liberty', and C. G. MacCallum 'Negative and Positive Freedom'. For a political view of liberty in some respects close to Nozick's, see F. von Hayek, *The Constitution of Liberty*. That the free market is necessary for liberty has also been argued by M. Friedman, in *Capitalism and Freedom*. Also see M. Friedman and R. Friedman, *Free to Choose*. For discussion of this, and related issues, see A. Buchanan, *Ethics, Efficiency, and the Market*. More specifically addressed to Nozick is H. Varian, 'Distributive Justice, Welfare Economics, and the Theory of Fairness'. D. Miller, in *Market, State, and Community*, has recently argued that it is possible to combine the market with socialism.

The relation between exploitation, the market, and capitalism is discussed in a number of papers collected in *Modern Theories of Exploitation*, edited by A. Reeve. The standard Marxist view is argued by N. Holstrom, in 'Exploitation'. For important criticism of the standard marxist account, see G. A. Cohen, 'The Labour Theory of Value and the Concept of Exploitation'. A modified Marxist view, which connects the theories of exploitation and alienation, is put forward by A. Buchanan, 'Exploitation, Alienation, and Injustice'. J. Roemer's work on exploitation has also proved highly influential. See, in particular, *A General Theory of Exploitation and Class*, and 'Should Marxists Be Interested in Exploitation?'.

In opposition to Nozick, a number of writers have attempted to rehabilitate the theory of distributive justice. Rawls partially replies to Nozick in 'The Basic Structure as Subject'. Others have adopted versions of the contractualist approach. For very different applications see T. Scanlon, 'Contractualism and Utilitarianism', and D. Gauthier, *Morals by Agreement*. B. Barry, *Theories of Justice*, is a detailed, recent, discussion.

On the topic of equality, B. Williams, 'The Idea of Equality', and T. Nagel, 'Equality', are two influential contemporary papers. The case for equality has recently been put very clearly by J. Baker, in *Arguing for Equality*, while the case against has been put by J. R. Lucas in 'Against Equality', and 'Against Equality Again'. Many current discussions take as their starting point two papers by R. Dworkin: 'What is Equality? Part 1: Equality of Welfare'; and 'What is Equality? Part 2: Equality of Resources'. In the latter of these, Dworkin claims that his theory of equality is resistant to Nozick's 'Wilt Chamberlain' argument. Hume's discussion of equality and desert, from his *Enquiry Concerning the Principles of Morals*, Section III, Part 1, is very highly recommended. The best recent work devoted to the topic of desert is G. Sher, *Desert*.

Nozick himself has added little to the debate on the justice of libertarianism. However, the earlier paper 'Coercion' is, in some respects, a preliminary study to *Anarchy, State, and Utopia*. *Philosophical Explanations* contains a number of chapters on ethics, but very little has any direct relevance to libertarian themes. In *The Examined Life* Nozick briefly indicates that he has given up some of this earlier views, and he makes some suggestions about a just scheme of inheritance taxation. As Nozick there says, now he is no longer a libertarian.

Bibliography

Works by Robert Nozick

'Coercion', in *Philosophy, Politics and Society*, 4th ser., ed. P. Laslett, W. G. Runciman, and Q. Skinner (Blackwell, Oxford, 1972), pp. 101–35.
Anarchy, State, and Utopia (Blackwell, Oxford, 1974).
'Who Would Choose Socialism?', *Reason* (May 1978), pp. 22–3.
Philosophical Explanations (Oxford University Press, Oxford, 1981).
'On The Randian Argument', in *Reading Nozick*, ed. J. Paul (Blackwell, Oxford, 1982), pp. 206–31.
The Examined Life (Simon and Schuster, New York, 1989).

Other Works Cited

Altham, J. E. J., 'Reflections on the State of Nature', in *Rational Action* ed. R. Harrison (Cambridge University Press, Cambridge, 1980), pp. 133–46.
Baker, John, *Arguing for Equality* (Verso, London, 1987).
Barry, B., *Theories of Justice* (Harvester Wheatsheaf, London, 1989).
Barry, B., and Hardin, R. (ed.), *Rational Man and Irrational Society* (Sage, Beverly Hills, Calif., 1982).
Becker, L. C., *Property Rights* (Routledge & Kegan Paul, Boston, Mass., 1977).
Bentham, Jeremy, *An Introduction to the Principles of Morals and Legislation* (Methuen, London, 1982).
—— *Anarchical Fallacies*, in *Nonsense upon Stilts*, ed. Jeremy Waldron (Methuen, London, 1987), pp. 46–76.

Berlin, Isaiah, 'Two Concepts of Liberty', in his *Four Essays on Liberty* (Oxford University Press, Oxford, 1969), pp. 118–72.

Braverman, Henry, *Labour and Monopoly Capitalism* (Monthly Review Press, New York, 1984).

Buchanan, A., 'Exploitation, Alienation, and Injustice', *Canadian Journal of Philosophy*, 9 (1979), pp. 121–39.

—— *Ethics, Efficiency and the Market* (Rowman and Allanheld, Totowa, NJ, 1985).

Carter, A., *The Philosophical Foundations of Property Rights* (Harvester Wheatsheaf, New York, 1988).

Cohen, G. A., 'Robert Nozick and Wilt Chamberlain: How Patterns Preserve Liberty', *Erkenntis*, 11 (1977), pp. 5–23.

—— 'Illusions about Private Property and Freedom', in *Issues in Marxist Philosophy*, vol. 4, ed. J. Mepham and D.-H. Ruben (Harvester, Brighton, 1981), pp. 223–42.

—— 'Marx and Locke on Land and Labour', *Proceedings of the British Academy*, 71 (1985), pp. 357–88.

—— 'Self-Ownership, World-Ownership and Equality', in *Justice and Equality Here and Now*, ed. F. S. Lucash (Cornell University Press, Ithaca, NY, 1986), pp. 108–35.

—— 'Self-Ownership, World-Ownership and Equality: Part II', in *Social Philosophy and Policy*, 3 (1986), pp. 77–96.

—— *History, Labour, and Freedom* (Oxford University Press, Oxford, 1988).

—— 'The Labour Theory of Value and the Concept of Exploitation', in *History, Labour, and Freedom*, pp. 209–38.

—— 'The Structure of Proletarian Unfreedom', in *History, Labour, and Freedom*, pp. 255–85.

—— 'Freedom, Justice, and Capitalism', in *History, Labour, and Freedom*, pp. 286–304.

—— 'On The Currency of Egalitarian Justice', *Ethics*, 99 (1989), pp. 906–44.

Daniels, N. (ed.), *Reading Rawls* (Blackwell, Oxford, 1975).

Dworkin, R., *Taking Rights Seriously* (Duckworth, London, 1977).

—— 'What Is Equality?, Part 1: Equality of Welfare', *Philosophy and Public Affairs*, 10 (1981), pp. 185–246.

—— 'What Is Equality?, Part 2: Equality of Resources', *Philosophy and Public Affairs*, 10 (1981), pp. 283–345.

—— 'Liberalism', in his *A Matter of Principle* (Harvard University Press, Cambridge, Mass., 1985), pp. 181–204.

Elster, J., *Making Sense of Marx* (Cambridge University Press, Cambridge, 1985).

Friedman, M., *Capitalism and Freedom* (Chicago University Press, Chicago, Ill., 1962).

Friedman, M., and Friedman, R., *Free to Choose* (Penguin, Harmondsworth, Middlesex, 1980).

Gauthier, D., *Morals by Agreement* (Oxford University Press, Oxford, 1986).

Geras, N., 'The Controversy about Marx and Justice', in *Marxist Theory*, ed. A. Callinicos (Oxford University Press, Oxford, 1989), pp. 211–67.

Gibbard, A., 'Natural Property Rights', *Nous*, 10 (1976), pp. 77–86.

Grunebaum, J. O., *Private Ownership* (Routledge & Kegan Paul, London, 1987).

Gutmann, A., 'Communitarian Critics of Liberalism, *Philosophy and Public Affairs*, 14 (1985), pp. 308–22.

Hare, R. M., *Moral Thinking* (Oxford University Press, Oxford, 1981).

Harris, John, 'The Survival Lottery', *Philosophy*, 50 (1977), pp. 81–7.

Hart, H. L. A., 'Between Utility and Rights', in *The Idea of Freedom*, ed. A. Ryan (Oxford University Press, Oxford, 1979), pp. 77–98.

—— 'Are There Any Natural Rights?', in *Theories of Rights*, ed. J. Waldron (Oxford University Press, Oxford, 1984), pp. 77–90.

Hayek, F. von, *The Constitution of Liberty* (Routledge & Kegan Paul, London, 1960).

Heller, Joseph, *Picture This* (Macmillan, London, 1988).

Hempel, C. G., *Aspects of Scientific Explanation* (Free Press, New York, 1965).

Hirsch, F., *Social Limits to Growth* (Harvard University Press, Cambridge, Mass., 1976).

Hobbes, Thomas, *Leviathan*, ed. C. B. Macpherson (Penguin, Harmondsworth, Middlesex, 1968).

Hodgson, G., *Capitalism, Value and Exploitation* (Martin Robertson, Oxford, 1982).

Holmes, Robert, 'Nozick on Anarchism', in *Reading Nozick*, ed. J. Paul (Blackwell, Oxford, 1982), pp. 57–67.

Holstrom, Nancy, 'Exploitation', *Canadian Journal of Philosophy*, 7 (1977), pp. 353–69.

Honore, A. M., 'Ownership', in *Oxford Essays in Jurisprudence*, ed. A. G. Guest (Oxford University Press, London, 1961), pp. 107–47.

Hume, David, *Enquiries*, 3rd edn., ed. Selby-Bigge (Oxford University Press, Oxford, 1975).

—— 'Of the Original Contract', in his *Essays Moral Political and Literary*, ed. E. F. Miller (Liberty Press, Indianapolis, Ind., 1985), pp. 465–87.

Kant, I., *Groundwork of the Metaphysic of Morals*, in H. J. Paton, *The Moral Law* (Hutchinson, London, 1948).

Kavka, G. S., 'An Internal Critique of Nozick's Entitlement Theory', *Pacific Philosophical Quarterly*, 63 (1982), pp. 371–80.

Kirk, Russell, *The Conservative Mind* (Henry Regnery, Chicago, Ill., 1953).

Kirzner, Israel M., 'Entrepreneurship, Entitlement, and Economic Justice', in *Reading Nozick*, ed. J. Paul (Blackwell, Oxford, 1982), pp. 383–411.

Kuflik, A., 'Process and End-State in the Theory of Economic Justice', *Social Theory and Practice*, 8 (1982), pp. 73–94.

Lloyd Thomas, David, *In Defence of Liberalism* (Blackwell, Oxford, 1988).

Locke, John, *Two Treatises on Civil Government* (Cambridge University Press, Cambridge, 1960).

Lucas, J. R., 'Against Equality', *Philosophy*, 40 (1965), pp. 296–307.

—— 'Against Equality Again', *Philosophy*, 52 (1977), pp. 255–80.

Lukes, Stephen, *Marxism and Morality* (Oxford University Press, Oxford, 1987).

Lyons, David, 'The New Indian Claims and Original Rights to Land', in *Reading Nozick*, ed. J. Paul (Blackwell, Oxford, 1982), pp. 355–79.

MacCullum, G. G., 'Negative and Positive Freedom', *Philosophical Review*, 76 (1967), pp. 312–34.

Macpherson, C. B., 'Elegant Tombstones: A Note on Friedman's Freedoms', in his *Democratic Theory: Essays in Retrieval* (Oxford University Press, Oxford, 1973), pp. 143–56.

Manuel, F. E., and Manuel, F. P., *Utopian Thought in the Western World* (Blackwell, Oxford, 1979).

Mill, J. S., *Utilitarianism*, ed. Mary Warnock (Collins, Glasgow, 1962).

—— *On Liberty*, in *Utilitarianism*, pp. 126–250.

—— 'Bentham', in *Utilitarianism*, pp. 78–125.

Miller, David, *Social Justice* (Oxford University Press, Oxford, 1976).

—— *Anarchism* (Dent, London, 1984).

—— *Market, State, and Community* (Oxford University Press, Oxford, 1989).

Nagel, Thomas, 'Equality', in his *Mortal Questions* (Cambridge University Press, Cambridge, 1979), pp. 106–127.

—— 'The Fragmentation of Value', in *Mortal Questions*, pp. 128–41.

—— 'Libertarianism without Foundations', in *Reading Nozick*, ed. J. Paul (Blackwell, Oxford, 1982), pp. 191–205.

Nove, Alec, *The Economics of Feasible Socialism* (George Allen & Unwin, London, 1983).

Olivecrona, K., 'Locke's Theory of Appropriation', *Philosophical Quarterly*, 24 (1974), pp. 220–34.

O'Neill, O., 'The Most Extensive Liberty', *Proceedings of the Aristotelian Society*, 80 (1979/80), pp. 45–59.

—— 'Nozick's Entitlements', in *Reading Nozick*, ed. J. Paul, (Blackwell, Oxford, 1982), pp. 305–22.

—— 'The Great Maxims of Justice and Charity', in her *Constructions of Reason* (Cambridge University Press, Cambridge, 1989), pp. 219–33.

Paul, Jeffrey (ed.), *Reading Nozick* (Blackwell, Oxford, 1982).

—— 'The Withering of Nozick's Minimal State', in *Reading Nozick*, pp. 68–76.

Pen, J. *Income Distribution* (Penguin, Harmondsworth, Middlesex, 1971).

Quest, E., 'Whatever Arises from a Just Distribution by Just Steps Is Itself Just', *Analysis*, 37 (1977), pp. 204–8.

Rand, Ayn, *The Fountainhead* (New American Library, New York, 1952).

Rawls, John, *A Theory of Justice* (Oxford University Press, Oxford, 1972).

—— 'The Basic Structure as Subject', *American Philosophical Quarterly*, 14 (1977), pp. 159–65.

—— 'Kantian Constructivism in Moral Theory', *Journal of Philosophy*, 77 (1980), pp. 515–72.

—— 'Social Unity and Primary Goods', in *Utilitarianism and Beyond*, ed. Amartya Sen and Bernard Williams (Cambridge University Press, Cambridge, 1982), pp. 159–85.

—— 'Justice as Fairness: Political not Metaphysical', *Philosophy and Public Affairs*, 14 (1985), pp. 223–51.

Reeve, Andrew, *Property* (Macmillan, London, 1986).

—— (ed.), *Modern Theories of Exploitation* (Sage, London, 1987).

Roemer, J., *A General Theory of Exploitation and Class* (Harvard University Press, Cambridge, Mass., 1982).

—— 'Should Marxists Be Interested in Exploitation?', in *Analytical Marxism*, ed. J. Roemer (Cambridge University Press, Cambridge, 1986), pp. 260–83.

Rothbard, Murray N., *The Ethics of Liberty* (Humanities Press, Atlantic Highlands, NJ, 1982).

Rousseau, Jean-Jacques, *The Social Contract* (Penguin, Harmondsworth, Middlesex, 1968).

—— *A Discourse on Inequality* (Penguin, Harmondsworth, Middlesex, 1984).

Russell, Bertrand, *Political Ideals* (George Allen & Unwin, London, 1963).

Russell, Paul, 'Nozick, Need and Charity', *Journal of Applied Philosophy*, 4 (1987), pp. 205–16.

Ryan, Alan, *Property and Political Theory* (Blackwell, Oxford, 1984).

—— *Property* (Open University Press, Milton Keynes, 1987).

Ryan, Cheyney, 'Yours, Mine and Ours: Property Rights and Individual Liberty', in *Reading Nozick*, ed. J. Paul (Blackwell, Oxford, 1982, pp. 323–43.

Sachs, D., 'How to Distinguish Self-Respect from Self-Esteem', *Philosophy and Public Affairs*, 10 (1981), pp. 346–60.

Sandel, M., *Liberalism and the Limits of Justice* (Cambridge University Press, Cambridge, 1982).

Scanlon, T., 'Contractualism and Utilitarianism', in *Utilitarianism and Beyond*, ed. Amartya Sen and Bernard Williams (Cambridge University Press, Cambridge, 1982), pp. 103–28.

—— 'Nozick on Rights, Liberty, and Property', in *Reading Nozick*, ed. J. Paul (Blackwell, Oxford, 1982), pp. 107–29.

—— 'The Significance of Choice', in *The Tanner Lectures on Human Values*, vol. 7, ed. S. McMurry (University of Utah Press, Salt Lake City, Utah, 1988), pp. 151–216.

Scheffler, S., 'Natural Rights, Equality, and the Minimal State', in *Reading Nozick*, ed. J. Paul (Blackwell, Oxford, 1982), pp. 148–68.

Schlatter, R., *Private Property, History of an Idea* (George Allen & Unwin, London, 1951).

Scruton, Roger, *The Meaning of Conservatism* (Macmillan, London, 1984).

Sen, Amartya, 'Rational Fools', in *Philosophy and Economic Theory*, ed. F. Hahn and M. Hollis (Oxford University Press, Oxford, 1977), pp. 87–109.

—— 'Rights and Agency', *Philosophy and Public Affairs*, 11 (1982), pp. 3–39.

Sher, G., *Desert* (Princeton University Press, Princeton, NJ, 1987).

Shue, H., *Basic Rights* (Princeton University Press, Princeton, NJ, 1980).

Sidgwick, Henry, *The Methods of Ethics* (Macmillan, London, 1907).

Simmons, A. John, *Moral Principles and Political Obligations* (Princeton University Press, Princeton, NJ, 1979).

Singer, Peter, 'The Right to be Rich or Poor', in *Reading Nozick*, ed. J. Paul (Blackwell, Oxford, 1982), pp. 37–53.

Skillen, Anthony, *Ruling Illusions* (Harvester, Hassocks, Sussex, 1977).

Smart, J. J. C., and Williams, B., *Utilitarianism, For and Against* (Cambridge University Press, Cambridge, 1973).

Spencer, Herbert, *Social Statics* (Chapman, London, 1851).

Steiner, Hillel, 'The Structure of a Set of Compossible Rights', *Journal of Philosophy*, 74 (1977), pp. 767–75.

—— 'The Natural Right to the Means of Production', *Philosophical Quarterly*, 27 (1977), pp. 41–9.

—— 'Liberty and Equality', *Political Studies*, 29 (1981), pp. 555–69.

—— 'Land, Liberty, and the Early Herbert Spencer', *History of Political Thought*, 3 (1982), pp. 515–33.

—— 'Justice and Entitlement', in *Reading Nozick*, ed. J. Paul, (1982), pp. 380–2.

Sweezy, Paul M., *The Theory of Capitalist Development* (Monthly Review Press, New York, 1942).

Taylor, Charles, 'What's Wrong with Negative Liberty?', in his *Philosophy and the Human Sciences*, Philosophical Papers vol. 2 (Cambridge University Press, Cambridge, 1985), pp. 211–29.

—— 'The Diversity of Goods', in *Philosophy and the Human Sciences*, pp. 230–47.

Theirs, Adolphe, *De la propriété* (Paris, 1848), cited in R. Schlatter, *Private Property, History of an Idea* (George Allen & Unwin, London, 1951), p. 236.

Thomson, J. J., 'Some Ruminations on Rights', in *Reading Nozick*, ed. J. Paul (Blackwell, Oxford, 1982), pp. 130–47.

Tuck, R., *Natural Rights Theories: Their Origin and Development* (Cambridge University Press, Cambridge, 1979).

Tucker, Benjamin, *State Socialism and Anarchy* (first published in 1888), in *The Anarchist Reader*, ed. G. Woodcock (Fontana, Glasgow, 1977), pp. 143–52.

—— *Instead of a Book* (B. R. Tucker, New York, 1893).

van der Veen, R., and Van Parijs, P., 'Entitlement Theories of Justice: From Nozick to Roemer and Beyond', *Economics and Philosophy*, 1 (1985), pp. 69–81.

Varian, Hal, 'Distributive Justice, Welfare Economics, and the Theory of Fairness', *Philosophy and Public Affairs*, 4 (1974), pp. 223–47.

Waldron, Jeremy (ed.), *Theories of Rights* (Oxford University Press, Oxford, 1984).

—— (ed.), *Nonsense upon Stilts* (Methuen, London, 1987).

—— *The Right to Private Property* (Oxford University Press, Oxford, 1988).

Walzer, Michael, *Spheres of Justice* (Blackwell, Oxford, 1983).

Williams, Bernard, 'The Idea of Equality', in his *Problems of the Self* (Cambridge University Press, Cambridge, 1973), pp. 230–65.

—— 'Conflicts of Values', in his *Moral Luck* (Cambridge University Press, Cambridge, 1981), pp. 71–82.

—— 'The Minimal State', in *Reading Nozick*, ed. J. Paul (Blackwell, Oxford, 1982), pp. 27–36.

Wolff, J., 'What is the Problem of Political Obligation?' *Proceedings of the Aristotelian Society*, 91 (1990–1), forthcoming.

Wolff, R. P., *In Defense of Anarchism* (Harper, New York, 1973).

—— 'Robert Nozick's Derivation of the Minimal State', in *Reading Nozick*, ed. J. Paul (Blackwell, Oxford, 1982), pp. 77–104.

Woodcock, George, *The Anarchist Reader* (Fontana, Glasgow, 1977).

Index

acquisition, justice in, 10, 77–8, 100–15, 117
administration of justice, 39, 43–4, 50
  see also rights, procedural
alienation, 127–9
Altham, J. E. J., 146
anarchist theory, 9, 16, 36
anarchy *see* state of nature
appropriation *see* acquisition, justice in
Aristotle, 28

Bakunin, M., 9
baselines, problem of, 112–15, 117
Bentham, J., 17, 24, 97

capitalism, 134, 152
  see also free market
Chaplin, C., 127
charity, 12, 32, 105, 111
Cohen, G. A., 87, 113, 144, 147, 151

compensation
  principle of, 67–70
  prohibition and, 52, 59–66
consent, 8
consent theory, 40–2, 47–8
  hypothetical, 50
  tacit, 41–2, 51
Conservatism, 136–8
current time-slice principles, *see* end-state principles

dependency culture, 33
desert, 70, 75, 120–2, 141
Dick, J., 150
difference principle *see* Rawls, J.
dirty hands, problem of, 21–2
distributive justice, 9–10, 73–117
  see also acquisition, justice in; entitlement theory of justice; rectification, justice in; transfer, justice in
divine rights of kings, 25

Printed in the United States
19370LVS00006B/166-264